Moving, funny, insightful… Some Miracles Need a Mom fits all three descriptors. Parenthood is not for the faint of heart. Mary is the most revered parent in history because her Son changed the world. It all started with a little push.

Paul Gunn | CEO, KUOG Corporation

As someone who believes in the power of prayer, I understand miracles take work. Not only does McKeown know this, she's written about her experiences and changed the way I look at Jesus's first miracle. I recommend this book to anyone patient enough to work for a miracle.

**Tamara Nall | CEO & Founder,
The Leading Niche**

Some Miracles Need a Mom exceeded my expectations! I picked up the book for pointers on how to help my kids out of the house, but I was blown away by the personal stories and how the author's faith in God and his promises sustained her through many trials. Emotional and accessible – consider this as a must-read for every book club!

**Tom Fedro | President & CEO, Paragon
Software Group Corporation, bestselling author
of Next Level Selling**

Some Miracles Need a Mom is a transformative read. It goes back to the beginning of Jesus's ministry and boils it down to a human level.

John Desilva | Master Mariner, and Author of 'Captain's Log Book'

Some

Miracles

Need a Mom

Sandy McKeown

CP

Published in the United States by Story Leaders.
www.leaderspress.com

ISBN 978-1-63735-100-0 (pbk)
ISBN 978-1-63735-101-7 (ebook)

SIMON &
SCHUSTER

Print Book Distributed by Simon & Schuster
1230 Avenue of the Americas
New York, NY 10020

Library of Congress Control Number: 2021919821
Cover design by Janet Wall, Wall2Wall Productions

Dedication

This book is dedicated to:

Julie Anderson, who never doubted this book would
be published, believed in this project
when my faith waivered, and never failed to
encourage me;

Lee **and** *Kathie Crum*, who unselfishly walked this
long and arduous journey described herein with our
family with unending love and patience;

and to

Mrs. Edna Anderson, my fifth grade teacher at
Sanford School, who was the first person
on this planet to voice her belief in my writing
ability. Her encouragement started
the spark of possibilities.

Table of Contents

Preface

Who am I to write a book? About miracles, no less!

I am a simple woman who stood her ground and fought for her family when . . .

- Natural tendencies and dreams for my children's futures were not matching up.
- Experts predicted bleak outcomes.
- The long road toward raising and then releasing adult children out into the cold, big world to live thriving, successful lives seemed so, so impossible.

I am a mom who ultimately realized she could not fight this battle alone and needed someone to fill in all her weaknesses.

"But he said to me, 'My grace is sufficient for you, for my power is made perfect in weakness.' Therefore I will boast all the more gladly about my weaknesses, so that Christ's power may rest on me."[1]

Let me boast: I have many weaknesses! But despite them all, my Lord, by his grace, used me to

---

[1] 2 Corinthians 12:9 New International Version (NIV) of the Bible

accomplish more than I ever dreamed possible for my family.

Another mom that was passionate about her family was Mary, the mother of Jesus. This book is also about her. Her loved ones ran out of wine at a wedding—and she did something about it. This story is not about the wine. It's about the pursuit of a miracle.

Mary knew what she could do, because she knew what her son could do. She knew she could ask for a miracle because, I believe, she had witnessed miracles in her own home, where the Son of Man was raised.

Turning water into wine at the wedding in Cana wasn't Jesus' *first* miracle. It was his first *public* miracle.

Miracles at home are private miracles—until someone tells you about them. In this book, I'm telling *you* about them. The miracle at Cana never would have happened without Mary. And I believe the multiple miracles in our home never would have happened without many prayers, leaning in closer to the Lord, and being obedient to his directives. Does that sound boastful? Perhaps. But imagine a mother bear fighting for her cubs. She doesn't care what her roar sounds like! And neither do I.

As you read this book, I pray you find the guidance and courage to fight like a momma bear with faith like Mary.

Please know that I did not come up with the concept for this book on my own. I felt strongly drawn to John 2:1-11. I found myself reading it over and over again, until finally, I called out: "What do you want from me, Lord?" I had already been directed, previously, to Jeremiah 30:2 (NIV), "This is what the Lord, the God of Israel, says: Write in a book all the words I have spoken to you." This book is a result of hearing and obeying what I believe the Lord asked me to do through these texts.

Honestly, it was easier to give birth five times, collectively, than to give birth to this one book. May you labor far less intensively as you read it. May this book empower you to boldly stand firm and fight for positive futures for your family. May you never feel hopeless. May you always know what the next step is to keep your family together, walking toward better futures and toward Jesus.

And may the pursuit of miracles be an ordinary part of your daily life.

For *your* family,
Sandy

1

They Have No More Wine

"Where did *that* come from?" I murmured to myself.

Standing in the doorway of the barn, my eyes adjusting from the dim light to the bright morning sunshine, I could see there was a strange black car parked in front of our farmhouse. I hadn't heard it arrive—and there was no one inside the car. It was eerie, so out of place. I quickly scanned the wide-open space between the house and the barn. I saw no one.

I was home alone—wearing baby doll pajamas, of all things—and not expecting visitors.

My parents had taken my younger sisters with them on a quick trip over the weekend. My older two siblings had already moved out. This was the first time I had been left alone to do the chores for more than a day. I woke up that morning, remembering right away it was time to do what I'd promised—feed the pigs. But, what to wear? I had washed every single piece of laundry in the house the night before. I didn't want to put on freshly washed jeans and a t-shirt just to have them stinking like pigs five minutes later, so I wore my pajamas. They needed washing anyway, so I paired them with my dad's oversized boots and trod out to the barn.

I'd finished the chores and was just about to exit the barn when I saw the unfamiliar car.

The house was unlocked, and I realized that whoever had driven that car must have taken the liberty of walking into the house. *Rude!*

It made me nervous. I felt unsafe and . . . um . . . a bit exposed.

Deciding that I needed a better vantage point, I quickly ran (as fast as I could in oversized boots—it was more of a sloppy half-trot) over to my parents' camper, which was parked nearby, while keeping an eye on the front door of the house. Once in the camper, I peeked through the window. There was still no sign of anyone.

I started frantically opening doors and drawers in the camper, looking for anything more appropriate to wear that might have been left behind after the last camping trip. I came across my brother's old high school letter jacket. I slipped that on over my now stinking-like-barn pajamas and stayed inside the camper, alert for any movement from the house. Watching for a stranger, feeling more and more terrified the longer the unknown remained unknown.

About a minute later, the door opened.

It was my fiancé.

Confused about why he was unexpectedly back in town early (he's a conductor on the railroad), I sheepishly climbed out of the camper and came around the corner into his view, wearing my morning barn attire.

His eyes widened when he saw me and asked, "*What* are you wearing?"

I shared my explanation and then demanded an explanation in return. I wanted to know about this car I'd never seen before!

He educated me on the latest aspect of his job, which I was trying to understand as his future wife. He kept this car in another city that he stayed in for work on his regular railroad run. There had been too many crews at the other end of the line this time, so higher-ups had sent some crews back by car instead of by train, he explained. It's called deadheading, he added.

He hadn't called to tell me he was coming back to town early because he had wanted to surprise me. He did do that!

I developed a new life-long phobia that day: I don't like surprises.

I excused myself, got out of those smelly pajamas, and took a shower. After getting properly dressed, my fiancé and I went for a ride in his black car from another city. But I will always remember how embarrassed I felt coming around the corner of the camper, wearing delicate pink, frilly, baby doll pajamas under an older, somewhat tattered letter jacket paired with spattered barn boots!

I had been quite content with my attire when it was just me and the pigs, alone in the darkness of the barn. But when my fiancé arrived, it changed my comfort level. The light of day and the views of others often change our comfort level.

Sometimes life's events develop into embarrassing situations.

Mary, the mother of Jesus, recognized when people she loved were facing an embarrassing situation.

According to the second chapter of John, Mary approached Jesus about a need at the wedding in Cana. She discovered that the ultimate faux pas at any wedding reception had occurred: the guests had nothing to drink.

"They have no wine,"[2] she said to Jesus. She recognized a problem and was doing something about it.

It's written that Mary was "there," not "called there" as Jesus and his disciples were. This suggests she was at her own home or at the home of a relative. She most likely would have been helping to serve at the festivities.

There is a certain protocol in weddings that has been true for ages: watch the "I do's," then enjoy refreshments.

In biblical times, marriage feasts lasted several days. This shortage of wine may have occurred on the third day of the feast, as mentioned in the first verse, with as many as four days to go. As water purification was not yet available, wine, a fermented drink, was the

---

[2] John 2:3b English Standard Version (ESV) of the Bible

customary choice. You can't host a wedding reception without something to drink for the guests.

Once, while serving as a coordinator for a wedding, I had to approach the parents of the bride immediately after the ceremony and give them the bad news: "The caterers failed to bring punch to serve at the reception," I whispered.

Both parents grimaced . . . and the three of us—having recognized the problem—began searching for an answer to the dilemma, while quietly praying for a solution. We could feel the pressure. A church full of people would soon be entering the reception hall thirsty.

As we searched and prayed, a solution was quickly found. However, there was no turning water into wine at this wedding. Iced tea was available for the thirsty on this summer day. Afterwards, I realized I had felt a little of what Mary probably felt at the wedding in Cana: the embarrassment, the anxiety.

Yet, the lack of wine at a wedding may seem like such a trivial dilemma. We all experience much bigger problems in our lives than what to serve our guests at a party. But, at some point, we are all looking for some kind of miracle in our lives.

My fiancé and I married the following summer. Thankfully, we didn't have any major problems at our wedding. It was after we started bringing babies home from the hospital that our bigger problems started. That's when our pursuit of miracles really began.

The Family

I met my future husband when I was just a teenager. The man I will refer to as the Conductor had become best friends with my brother. My brother had four sisters; the Conductor had six. They seemed to bond over this phenomenon.

My brother brought the Conductor out to the farm one day, introduced him to my parents and then, with a sweeping arm toward us four girls sprawled throughout the living room watching TV, said, "And they're my sisters."

The Conductor soon treated us just like his own sisters, teasing us and picking on us. One day while at the farm, he wiped out on the gravel with my brother's new motorcycle. My brother started running toward him, yelling, "If you're not dead, I'm going to kill you!"

As he limped toward the house with his minor injuries, I voiced my own lack of sympathy, "Serves you right."

He said it was the moment he decided he should be nicer to me.

And being nicer led to other things . . .

Our first child was born fourteen months after our wedding day. We barely knew what it was like to be married yet.

Our firstborn, who I'll call Leader, is a natural leader and problem solver. One day, one of his siblings spilled juice in the front entryway. I was on my way to sop up the mess when I witnessed the Leader do something, as a four-year-old, that stopped me midstride. I just stood there—in awe. I watched as he rolled the entry rug away from the spill that was running toward it. Where did he get that idea? I hadn't thought of it myself!

I was stunned at his quick thinking and the wisdom beyond his years that was revealed in that moment.

Our second child, who I'll call Wanderer, began exploring when he was only four years old. He was strong for his age and already riding a two-wheeled bike without training wheels. He would whip around the neighborhood until he got bored with it and then begin wandering. We'd put out the all-points bulletin to the neighborhood: *We've lost our Wanderer again.* And everyone would come out of their houses and start searching for him.

Our Wanderer had no fear. He was always amazingly calm, whatever was going on around him.

Our third child, Justice, was born with eyes wide open and alert. When his dad passed his hospital bassinet, his newborn eyes tracked him. Most newborns don't do that! Our Justice was always watching, observing, and asking questions.

As Justice grew, he fought for fairness and often wanted to know the answer to life's "whys." He cornered me on our stairway one afternoon when I was pregnant with his younger sibling. One of his aunts was also pregnant at the time and so was his schoolteacher. He demanded to know where babies come from, and he wanted to know *now.* I built on the previous pieces of information I'd shared with him, gave him the rest of the story, and kind of asked, *all good?* He went upstairs to his room. I went downstairs, but then remembered something I needed to add. I went back upstairs and found him lying in the top bunk bed, his eyes staring at the ceiling as if in shock. I got his attention and said, "I forgot to tell you something. You can't go to school and tell your friends this. Their moms need to tell them." He said, "Don't worry, Mom, I won't. They wouldn't believe me anyhow."

Determined was born just fourteen months after Justice. He had a sweet disposition and didn't seem to mind all the chaos of our growing family. Our Determined loved to have everything color-coded and in order, and his bedroom would have passed the most stringent surprise inspections from the toughest commanders. He had an uncanny ability to remember numbers, and he picked up the saxophone as a child, determined to play it as often as he could.

Our Princess arrived seven years after Determined. The Conductor and I thought we were done having kids, but God had another idea. And it was a good idea. This time, while pregnant, I added an extra prayer: "Lord, it would be really nice to have *one* child that liked to read. Just one?" And he answered. Our Princess never sat still—was always busy doing something—unless she was reading. She carried a book everywhere she went.

A passion for reading does make a difference in life. Or, maybe, we just need more passion for life?

More passion for what matters in eternity, forgetting what matters only here on earth, what will someday all pass away. Being mindful of things other than what is happening right in the moment. We need to take care of our families with an eye on eternity.

It's not always easy to find that passion on our own. We often need help. Occasionally, we get gently nudged toward a passion—not for *our* life, but a passion for someone else's life.

Like our children's.

Parenting with Challenges

You can't tell what your kids are going to be like when they're babies. They're born with gifts but develop more talents as they grow and learn.

But problems develop along the way, too. It's the world we live in.

If problems are just opportunities for growth, our children's problems are definitely an opportunity for our growth as parents.

We learned that problems are also opportunities for prayer.

As the problems became more evident, we began to realize just how much prayer we would need throughout the coming years.

Our Wanderer couldn't sit still, had trouble concentrating, left our approved boundaries often, and couldn't be located on a regular basis. These symptoms arrived by the time he was four years old.

When he was five, I was working in the kitchen cleaning up after a meal, and *I thought* my husband had all the kids in the backyard with him. He came dashing through the back door, ran through the kitchen, and was running up the stairs before I could get in the question, "What's wrong?"

"(Wanderer) is on the roof!"

Unbeknownst to us, our Wanderer had taken the screen off the window in an upstairs bedroom and climbed out onto the dormer roof to see what he could see. My husband had spotted him from the yard and had immediately and calmly instructed him to get back inside. He didn't want to startle our son. But after issuing his carefully chosen words, he was doing his best-ever hundred-yard dash to retrieve the errant child. Had we ever *told* this child he wasn't supposed to climb out onto our steep-peaked, Tudor-style roof? No, it hadn't crossed our minds. But we did start praying more earnestly for God to protect our children . . . from *themselves.*

By the time our Wanderer was in fourth grade, sitting still in school and paying attention in class had become a major struggle. Seeking outside help, we were told our Wanderer had attention deficit disorder as well as a mood disorder. Also, he had bouts with depression. At the time, I didn't even know kids got depressed!

Our Determined child didn't sleep through the night for the first three years of his life, often waking up, screaming a heart-wrenching, terrified cry, twice a night. It took hours to get him back to sleep each time. He had dark circles under both eyes and wasn't eating well. He smiled once in a while, but rarely laughed, and screeched instead of developing language.

I took Determined to our family physician to figure out the cause of the sleepless nights. She informed us our son was experiencing night terrors. She also told us that our Determined was autistic. She predicted he would most likely never speak and would probably need to be institutionalized.

His medical records also declared: failure to thrive.

My son wasn't thriving.

Her advice for the sleepless nights: allow him to cry it out.

I carried our Determined to the parked caravan in the clinic parking lot where my husband was waiting with the other kids in a car that was bouncing to and fro due to the shenanigans of pent-up energies from waiting too long. I strapped Determined into his car seat, got into the front passenger seat, and let the tears flow. I informed the Conductor that we didn't get any easy answers for the sleep issues from the doctor, but what we did get was a diagnosis for our Determined: autism.

I continued to cry, and my husband reached out, put his hand on mine and said, "It's going to be okay."

We marry our opposites, right? Opposites, by mere definition, respond differently from each other.

My world was crashing. His world was going to be fine.

Educational personnel confirmed the diagnosis of autism, as did an expert in the field from another state. But no one would guarantee eventual positive outcomes for his life. At best, they suggested, he could *possibly* be able to work on an assembly line. At worst, he may never be independent and need to live in an institution.

Our Justice was having headaches. That was what our new family doctor told us. He said he'd probably outgrow them when he became a teenager, which was common for boys. There was nothing to worry about.

But he started driving when he became a teenager. One day while driving, he had what we called "an episode." He drove through a closed garage door at the end of a long driveway, mistaking it for a road.

Now we needed answers.

A neurosurgeon gave them: our Justice had epilepsy.

Our Justice, who always wanted to know the whys wasn't happy with this answer. As parents, our relationship with him suffered tremendously during this time. We again searched for solutions and a child psychologist answered this time, diagnosing Justice with oppositional defiance and depression. In addition, tests at school divulged he had a reading disability. Our Justice was facing unbelievable obstacles on several fronts!

What do you do when facing unbelievable obstacles?

Where do you turn when you don't know which way to turn?

Who can help you with your kids when you're feeling so small in the world, so powerless?

If we have a powerful Father to whom we can take our needs, why not do it? Do we go to God meekly, in effect, saying, "Um . . . excuse me. Would you mind . . . if you have some time . . . could you please . . . um . . . help my son?"

No! We need to know that we can stand before God and pray for our children with passion like that demonstrated by David in Psalm 4:1 (ESV):

Answer me when I call,
O God of my righteousness!
You have given me relief when I was in distress.
Be gracious to me and hear my prayer!

Regretfully, we sometimes forget about God.

Dwight L. Moody wrote this story of Frederick Douglas in *The Overcoming Life*: "The great slave orator once said in a mournful speech when things looked dark for his race, 'The white man is against us, governments are against us, the spirit of the times is against us. I see no hope for the colored race. I am full of sadness.' Just then a poor old . . . woman rose in the audience, and said, 'Frederick, is God dead?'"

I am convinced that "poor old woman" was a mom. This mom knew if we count all our problems instead of count on God, we would all stay consumed by our problems. She understood that it takes strong faith to make a difference in the lives of our loved ones. Fierce faith makes a fervent difference when we tap into a powerful, faithful God. We can't afford to forget about God when we want something different for our kids!

Fierce faith makes a fervent difference
when we tap into a powerful, faithful God.

#SomeMiraclesNeedAMom | #AuthorSMcKeown

We have an almighty Father within reach who can help us when circumstances feel hopeless. Do you believe? Matthew 21:22 (ESV) promises: "And whatever you ask in prayer, you will receive, if you have faith."

Mary, the mother of Jesus, believed. She pursued a miracle on behalf of people she loved. As we dig deeper into this story at Cana, we will witness the steps Mary took to pursue that miracle. As we watch her take those steps together, and as I share the steps I took for my family, it is my prayer you will feel empowered with passionate faith to follow in those footsteps and pursue miracles for your loved ones. You are the best person to do this for your family. I know because . . . some miracles need a mom.

What problems are you facing?

Are you accessing an all-powerful God on behalf of those problems?

If not, why not?

2

She Knew His Capabilities

What could Jesus do about the lack of wine at a wedding? And why would Mary bother him with such a trivial need? Does it really matter if there wasn't enough wine? Something needs to "trigger" us into realizing a problem is too big for us to handle on our own, that the needs are too great.

The "triggers" in our home were coming at us with speed.

Daily life had gradually become nearly unmanageable for my family.

I had been up all night, and I looked it. My hair hadn't been *close* to a comb for twenty-four hours. I was wearing a purple flannel nightgown my mother had given me, and there was so much material to this thing that it billowed in the wind when I moved. The first time I had come downstairs wearing it, my husband looked over the top of the newspaper he was reading and asked, "Didn't we camp in that last summer?"

The sun rose that morning, long after our toddler and I were up. The rest of the household soon followed. At the time, our little diaper-wearer had a rash, so I decided to take his diaper off to allow his bottom to "breathe." I was keeping a bleary eye on him in the living room when I heard a combination of strange sounds I didn't recognize coming from the kitchen. I jumped up to investigate and discovered our Wanderer was making a honey-and-butter sandwich for his school lunch. The fact that his choice was not a nutritious one barely registered: honey and butter were everywhere—smeared across the counter, dripped across the wooden floor, and spewed across the table nook at the other end of the kitchen.

I walked into the room, letting my son know I was extremely unhappy with his choices that morning. I was so tired, my filters were no longer functioning, and I was mad. I reacted rather than responded. I picked up the knife that lay on the kitchen table to inspect it. So much butter and honey coated the thing that I couldn't tell which end was the handle and which end was the blade. I looked at it in disgust and casually tossed it back onto the table.

And to my horror, it *bounced*. Although I didn't think my toss had been forceful, the knife had skipped once on the table and then bounced right through the window at the end of the nook, shattering the glass. I couldn't believe it. Shocked, I turned, and as my eyes shifted away from the accumulated mess in the kitchen, my brain kicked in. I remembered in that

18

moment that I had a diaperless child on the loose. I hurried back to the living room to check on him and discovered yet another disaster. While I had been in the kitchen, he had made a rather large deposit on the carpeted stairs. I was too beyond tired to process it all.

At this point, the Conductor, who had been away on a freight train run for almost three days, was arriving home. As he walked around the house to enter through the back door, our contractor neighbor had his crew of men building a deck in his backyard. They had heard the yelling and had seen the knife come flying out of the kitchen window. Our neighbor warned my husband in his baritone voice, "You don't want to go in there."

My husband mumbled something about feeling obligated, and bravely walked in.

Without even greeting me, he took in the chaos and said over the heads of clamoring children, "Why don't you go to bed?" I reminded him he had been up all night, too, to which he responded, "It looks like you need sleep worse than I do."

With *that* encouragement, I turned and, purple flannel flying, ran past the fresh deposit on the stairs and went straight to bed.

Four hours later, I awoke with a jolt. It was quiet downstairs. That worried me. I ran back down the stairs to find that my husband had taken the school-aged kids to school, cleaned up the various messes from the morning (the deposit on the steps had been cleared), and taped up the broken window. The kitchen was spotless. He had our two preschoolers playing quietly beside his chair as his head bobbed toward his chest. He was fighting to stay awake.

I approached and put my hand on his shoulder and quietly said, "Tag. It's your turn to sleep." With a kiss to my face and weary relief on his, off to bed he went.

This wasn't what I had in mind when I had stood beside him before a large gathering of witnesses years earlier and, starry-eyed, vowed, "I do."

When things are not going how you had planned, what can Jesus do?

Mary knew. She'd seen him in action before.

Life with the Son of God

Mary shared a home with the Son of God. Somewhere along the way, she probably had more than one imperfect moment, household accident, or other issue that caused a problem in her life. Chances are, her son stepped in to help. Maybe she reached for a kettle over the fire and it slipped, causing her to burn her hands as she tried to save the contents. If that happened, the hand of God would have been near. Did her son reach out and touch her wound to remove the sharp pain? If so, her awe might have caused her to wonder if the injury had ever happened at all . . . just for a moment. But she would have known from that instant: he healed.

After Joseph died, did Mary, as a poor carpenter's widow, go to her pantry one day only to find it empty? And when she circled around and back again, wondering what she would do next, did she find something to cook after all? I believe something like this most likely happened. Mary saw her son's capabilities several times during his early years. Her confidence in him at that wedding came from experience. She had lived with Jesus. She knew he performed miracles.

Mary had known this child was different from the start because of his highly unusual conception. An angel had simply told her how her pregnancy would come to be. But throughout the remaining years of his life, Jesus was a living example of "different."

Mary knew her son well. As we read in Luke 2:19 (ESV), she wisely "treasured up all these things, pondering them in her heart." After giving birth, she paused and wondered about all that had just happened. She was a virgin! And she just given birth to a beautiful son! These things don't go together! Surely this was something to think about! In Luke 2:40 (ESV) we see her watching as "the child grew and became strong." Most moms watch the amazing progression of our children growing, but Luke wrote about something that made Jesus stand out from his fellow Nazarene neighbor kids even more. He was: "filled with wisdom. And the favor of God was upon him." In Luke 2:48 (ESV), we read that after searching, along with Joseph, for three days for her twelve-year-old son, she asked after finding him, "Son, why have you treated us so? Behold, your father and I have been searching for you in great distress."

Jesus responded to his mother's inquiry, "Did you not know that I must be in my Father's house?."[3] Even at a young age, Jesus had his Father's work in mind. He was thinking of the mission he had for his life. He was thinking of the future. His mother was thinking of the current day.

While Jesus was still young, under Mary's motherly protection and care, she knew him. Yet, she didn't fully understand his role in the world beyond her four walls. She likely knew he had extraordinary healing powers and could save her from temporary pain, but did she know he could save her from eternal pain? I don't think she did, at least not at first.

Sometimes the world doesn't understand our children. It's our job, as moms, to understand them better than most.

Becoming Students of Our Children

Mary was a student of Jesus. Think about this. Mary had raised him in her home. She knew what he liked, what he didn't like. She knew what motivated him. She knew he was compassionate and helped those in need because she had experienced that help herself. She knew his character. She knew him because she had watched him, studied him, and learned from him.

If Mary was a student of her son, should we not follow suit?

I believe it's our job, as moms, to become students of our children.

---

[3] (Luke 2:49, ESV)

What makes our kids tick? How do they learn? What do they like? Why do they do the things that they do? If we understand our children in our homes today, we can help them function—and succeed—in the world tomorrow.

Many books are available to help us understand our kids better. I highly recommend Cynthia Ulrich Tobias' book *The Way They Learn*. This book will help you understand how your child processes information. Once we, as parents, can help our children learn in their own style, the world will be opened to them. When our children are learning to their utmost potential because we are reaching them in their specific learning style, their potential will explode.

We, as parents, need to get to know our children. We should try to find out the answers to questions like: how do they learn? How do they feel loved?

All children are different. They don't learn the same way. In *The Way They Learn*, Tobias discusses the four main learning styles and helps us identify them in our kids so we can teach in their style and to their strengths. Without this vital step, our children won't learn as well and their life choices for their future will be limited.

Mary most likely didn't understand how the all-knowing Son of God's thought processes worked. How could she? But she still understood his strengths. She understood his extraordinary character. She understood how he loved. Should we do less?

In *The Five Love Languages of Children*, Gary Chapman explains that there are different "love languages." If I attempt to love each of my children in the same manner, some will not feel loved because they don't all understand and receive love in the same manner. (Who said love isn't complicated?)

Reading books and putting the knowledge we learn from them to use is just one way we can understand our kids to the best of our ability. With the new tools we learn, we can then redirect, and feed them information in their learning languages, so our kids' best abilities eventually shine.

But sometimes your kids are doing things no one has written about yet.

When Determined was two, he would throw a tantrum when he didn't like something. He had no language skills at the time, and his understanding of our verbal communication was also limited. Tantrums were one of his primary ways of communicating.

One morning I took the kids to a local fast food restaurant to enjoy a treat and play at the indoor playground. Something upset Justice over by the play area and I was calming him down when I heard a commotion in the aisle on the other side of the restaurant. Determined had lain down in the middle of the restaurant and begun to kick and cry. I was en route to him when a stranger walked by, glanced down in disgust, and proclaimed, "Damn kids!" I'm unsure if she had missed her morning coffee, but I do remember feeling defensive for my son. I didn't muster the energy to explain; I didn't fully understand it myself at the time. He looked like he was behaving like a spoiled child. Onlookers certainly couldn't tell otherwise.

24

The multilayered issues occurring on a simple trip out in public with my children were mind-numbing to me. I knew the world touted individuality and trail blazers—those that are different—yet I was beginning to grapple with the fact that when my sons displayed characteristics outside the so-called "normal" boundaries, people weren't so thrilled.

I needed to find a way to communicate with this non-communicative son. I had discovered he was a visual learner. I needed to communicate with him in a visual manner.

It was a problem that I needed to figure out how to address. But first, I needed to pray.

Why Pray?

Why do we pray? I pray simply because I don't have all the answers. I look to a God who is bigger than me, one who can see a bigger picture. I have acquired certain life skills as a mom, but through time—and some agonizing experiences—I've discovered they aren't enough for me to handle every challenge that comes up with my kids.

While my husband was a teenager, he spent a weekend at a Minnesota lake with a family that included seven sons (God bless 'em! I can only imagine the commotion and chaos involved on a weekend getaway with that many boys).

On one particular day, one of the older boys was at the helm of the family's speedboat, and my future husband was skiing behind the boat. According to my husband, his friend didn't slow down for an upcoming turn, so my guy lost his skis and tumbled several times *on top of the water* before quickly sinking beneath the waves. When his downward momentum finally slowed, he began swimming toward the surface. He wasn't worried. He was both a lifeguard and a member of the swim team. He certainly had the skills to swim to the surface.

But the swim was more difficult than it should have been. He had to work too hard to reach the surface—and it wasn't getting any closer. Suddenly remembering he was wearing a life preserver, my rational athlete relaxed his body to allow the flotation device to do its job. To his amazement, his momentum immediately shifted—in the opposite direction from the one in which he had been swimming. Because he had tumbled so many times and because the lake was so murky, his senses had become confused. He literally didn't know which way was up! When he remembered to rely on his life preserver, his position in the water became clear. Only then did he make it to the surface safely.

Sometimes when we're in the midst of the trials of caring for challenging kids, it can be easy to get confused and forget "which way is up." We pour all of our energy into solutions that may be taking us in the wrong direction. Many people, in the midst of their confusion, refuse to rely on God, jeopardizing their very life! But if we remember the "life preserver" we have in Christ, and trust him, praying for his direction, he will gently lead us toward the surface. His vision is better than ours.

The Beginning of Change

When I reached this step of trusting my Lord rather than my own efforts, I began to pray: *Lord, please show me how to communicate with my non-communicative son.*

The unexpected answer I got was: "Buy more shoes!"

Truthfully, when I first heard this answer, I was a bit incredulous. Shoes? Really? This doesn't make any sense!

But my loving Father nudged me.

And I obeyed.

I bought shoes for Determined just to wear to church. I bought him shoes just for going to school. I bought him shoes just to wear while he played outdoors. And I bought him shoes just for doing errands and shopping. And then I was very, very careful to only put each pair of shoes on him for its assigned purpose. Why? I was trying to communicate nonverbally. The goal was to help him understand where he was going *before* he got there—which would, I hoped, reduce his public tantrums.

The first day I knew we were getting somewhere with this system was a huge milestone. Determined didn't like church at the time because we attended a large one that was very noisy, and his preschool class was appropriately geared toward the attention span of "normal" two-year-old children. The class transitioned often to new activities, which was difficult for my son; he didn't like having to switch gears. On several Sunday mornings, I had taken him

27

to his Sunday school room and held the door shut while he kicked and screamed on the other side of the door. I would direct other parents to use the alternate door while I stood there trying to hold my ground.

On this particular morning, Determined immediately started to throw a tantrum when I tried to put the first church shoe on his foot. It was an "ah-ha" moment. I knew that *he* knew what those shoes meant. He was getting the nonverbal message that he was going to church.

We wrestled on the floor, and I finally got those shoes on his wriggling feet. Afterwards, I stood up as he momentarily laid still on the floor in defeat, and I declared, "Tough. You're going anyway." And I walked away. As I walked away, he stopped crying. It was a victory! He had communicated in his style that he didn't want to go to church, and I had communicated in my style that he was going whether he wanted to go or not. And . . . I didn't sit around and coddle him. My husband was out of town again, and I had three other kids to get ready for church.

The shoe system was the beginning of our communicating, and the beginning of the end of Determined's tantrums. The shoe system was the first step we took towards achieving what we could for our Determined.

I began to understand our son. He had been diagnosed with autism, and communication was a big hurdle for him. However, he was a smart kid! His learning style was simply narrowly focused. He required countless more visual cues than other kids because his language skills were low. Even though my child has challenges, I believe with my whole heart that everything God created is good.[4] Our child may have a diagnosis of autism, but that doesn't mean he wasn't created for something extraordinary!

Because I prayed for wisdom in how to communicate with my son, I believe God answered, in turn helping me discover more fully the value of communicating with him. I was learning to lean more on my Father while beginning to understand my son.

The problems we were accumulating as a functioning family were altering the way our family functioned. I needed more of Jesus so I could be more for my family. Those memes on social media that proclaim: *Moms, you are enough* are a lie. I'm sorry, but we *aren't* enough. We need Jesus to fill in all those weak spots so we can be strong. Really strong for the storms of life, not just ho-hum strong. We need to learn to lean on God for unlimited and unimaginable capabilities beyond ours.

Just as Mary did.

We need more of Jesus so we can be more for our families.

#SomeMiraclesNeedAMom | #AuthorSMcKeown

---

[4] 1 Timothy 4:4 (ESV)

When a problem with our children confronts us in life, we don't stop and say, "Well, I guess that's the way it's going to be. We're just going to have to learn how to live with it." No! We don't stop there!

There's much more we can do for our kids.

Do you know the capabilities of your children?

Are you struggling with that?

Please pray this simple prayer: *Show me, Lord, how to understand and learn from my child.*

3

She Knew Her Capabilities

We moved to a different state when the Princess was thirteen years old. As she found new friends, and eventually built a solid relationship with a new best friend, I became good friends with this new friend's mom. She became a sort of "co-mom."

The girls did what kids do: they grew up and then went off to different colleges in different states, graduated, and found different jobs in different countries. However, once back home, the girls would get together as often as they could.

I received a surprising text from this co-mom one morning: "Do you know about our daughters' plans to go on an overnight trip with their boyfriends this weekend?"

I messaged back: "No, I did not! What's up with that?"

Now . . . I need to clarify. This best friend tells her mom *everything*. The Princess tells her dad and

I only what she has to. This mom knew more about what was going on in her daughter's life than I did, especially as her daughter was currently living with her. Our daughter lived forty minutes away in her own apartment. We weren't keeping track of her daily decisions.

But sometimes things come up that give you pause.

My co-mom went on: "I try to stay out of my adult kids' business, but when I *really* get concerned about something, I will muster the courage to say something."

I thought about this conversation for a total of five minutes.

Then I texted my daughter's boyfriend: "Hi! Can you give me a call when you have a moment, please?"

He called about thirty minutes later and we had a nice talk.

I then texted my co-mom back. "I just had a little chat with (the Princess's boyfriend). I informed him we raised the Princess to be a godly woman who would be a gift for a godly man on their wedding night. She is wearing a purity ring as a reminder. (He was aware of its significance). I asked him if he respected her. (He said he did and also respected us). I then told him he had not given us any reason to distrust him, so we choose to continue to trust him. And . . . to have a fun, godly weekend."

These girls were both twenty-three years old at the time of this conversation. We needed to have confidence in how we had raised them. But both families were also still getting to know the boyfriends.

You don't just throw your daughters to wolves! You watch and make sure they're with godly gentlemen who make good choices.

At the very least, the Princess' boyfriend would hear my words echoing in his head throughout the weekend, right? (I prayed it would be so!)

My kids rolled their eyes and exclaimed, "Only our mom would do that!"

And my glib response was, "That's right!"

They tease me for asking the hard questions, but I'm quite sure I'm not the only one who asks them. I know several moms that, when presented with something questionable at first glance, have doubts of their own. "What's up with that?" is not out of the ordinary!

I was given five kids to rear. Being a parent doesn't stop because your kids become "legal" adults. For the record, my daughter was more emotionally mature than a lot of adults I know long before she turned eighteen.

But I'm still her mother.

My talking to a man who was dating my daughter about his intentions toward my daughter was not out of line. Period. Hoping he heard that conversation echoing in his mind was not emotional warfare from his girlfriend's mother—it was a spiritual prompt from his heavenly Father!

Did I have a hand in conveying to him our family's stance—and God's—to the rights and wrongs in this matter? Unabashedly so.

As a mom, I have the capability to influence right choices my kids are making. I am not a passive mother. And my passion for the rights and wrongs in life—what my kids are choosing to do—didn't stop once they became adults.

Mary wasn't addressing a young son, she was addressing an adult son. And she wasn't a passive mother either. She knew she had the capability to influence her adult son.

She wasn't a wallflower that stood by at the wedding in Cana, worrying that there was no wine and not knowing what action to take.

She knew she could do something about it. Her son needed a nudge in the right direction, this she was sure of!

Likewise, I have never been a shy wallflower where my kids are concerned. I did something about the issues they were facing. I spoke up.

Ultimately, the Princess, her best friend, and their boyfriends decided *not* to go out-of-town for the whole weekend. That was *their* decision. Instead, they went for one day, driving to their destination in the early morning and driving back at night. Do I think we moms had an influence on that decision? Perhaps. My daughter told me the weather forecasters predicted heavy rain for the entire weekend—which, by the way, never developed. I believe our mom influence was extended through our prayers: *Lord, please help them make wise decisions.* He didn't send rain, but the *threat* of it was enough to alter their course.

Decisions alter our course in life.

Mary made a decision that changed lives at that wedding.

When Mary discovered the lack of wine at the wedding, she probably traveled from a preparation area, where the wine would be served from, to where Jesus was sitting with other men. Today, we can't walk toward the physical form of Jesus to address a need we may have. When we're unsure of what to do as mothers, we can still go to God. But, we may also rely heavily on the example of other mothers. But we need to choose these examples wisely.

One sister-in-law, whom I admire, is what I would call a "pit bull" mom—a woman who fights relentlessly for her kids and what she believes is right for them. Today's readers would probably call her a "tiger mom." She is someone in my sphere of influence who I have watched parent with deep passion and clarity. I didn't wear a bracelet asking, "What would Jesus do?" Instead, my mantra became, "What would Debbie do?" I couldn't see Jesus, but I could see Debbie. I needed to follow someone with skin, so to speak. I chose her.

Debbie's example gave me the courage to become a strong advocate for my children. When educators suggested putting our newly diagnosed two-year-old on a bus to travel across town and spend the day with other special needs kids, I had the strength to say no. Let me add, *this is what I felt was best for our child*. I am not saying this is what would be best for *every* autistic child. I just felt that I could better help our son at home.

Of course, the dissension came.

"Sandy, you will be wasting valuable time."

"He may never reach his full potential."

"You have three other kids (at the time). You are exhausted and depressed, and your husband travels out of town for work. It would be unwise to keep him at home."

I thanked all of these dissenters for their concerns and forged ahead, because I felt it was the right decision for us.

Similarly, when Mary spoke to Jesus, she demonstrated that she had taken ownership of the problem. She felt compelled to get involved.

She could have sat quietly with the other women, not moving or saying anything. She could have watched and done nothing. But she didn't waste the opportunity to make a difference. Was it a life-or-death situation? No. But it would have caused problems and possibly serious dishonor to the host family if they had no wine for their guests.

Don't waste an opportunity to make a difference for your kids.

#SomeMiraclesNeedAMom | #AuthorSMcKeown

Mary went to the man she thought could do something about the problem at hand. And, please note, she did it without blaming anyone.

Historians tell us that guests often brought wine to help the host family with the wedding expenses back in the days when Jesus walked the earth. If freeloaders outnumbered contributors, it was a sign of dishonor and a social slight on the family. According to the account in John, Mary didn't bring up the subject. She knew there was a problem; she didn't address the reason why.

Too often in today's culture, we fall into a trap of chasing cause. When we do, our first question is *Whose fault is it?* When we focus on assigning blame, we aren't focusing on understanding the problem and working toward a solution.

Why do our children disobey? Why do they develop conflicting attitudes? Why do they become defiant and unruly? We can spend a lot of time searching for these answers and pursuing a cause or blaming an establishment.

Mary used her time to solve the problem, not to blame anyone. She didn't settle for the circumstances at hand, but she didn't point fingers either. I believe that *in most cases* the problem's cause doesn't matter. For *me*, as a parent, pursuing a cause in a vindictive manner is not worth my time.

I only have twenty-four hours in the day. I have learned it's best to try to pour my energy into discovering solutions.

Mary knew this, as well.

Jesus had a choice at that wedding, and Mary knew she had the capability to influence that decision.

Mary wasn't afraid to speak up for what she believed was right. Too often fear paralyzes us. But we can't allow fear to stifle our petitions for our family.

The best way we can stop being fearful is to focus on the Word of God.

#SomeMiraclesNeedAMom | #AuthorSMcKeown

Mary Knew the Word

The first line of the book of John is: "In the beginning was the Word, and the Word was with God, and the Word was God."[5] Further on, in verse 14, we read, "And the Word became flesh and dwelt among us . . ."[6]

This Word that "became flesh" was Mary's son. The Son of Man doesn't walk on this earth in our lifetime, but we can still get to know him to the best of our ability by reading the information divinely given to us—the Bible. We, as parents, need to know the Son of Man and his characteristics so we can fully help our children. It is vital to understand his love for us and all that it entails to help us engage in the journey of parenthood.

---

[5] John 1:1 *The Holy Bible*, English Standard Version (ESV) (2016). Accessed via BibleGateway.com, Zondervan.
[6] John 1:14a (ESV)

It is good and right to respect God. But we can also approach him with confidence. Mary did. She didn't fear going to him with a request. She knew it was within her capabilities to do so.

And because she did, she ultimately changed the Son of God's mind. Think about that for a moment! *Mary knew she could change God's mind.* Because she had a personal relationship with the Son of God, she knew she could ask him to change course. This wasn't the first time something like this had happened.

God had plans for the Israelites. "And the Lord said to Moses, 'I have seen these people, and behold, it is a stiff-necked people. Now therefore let me alone, that my wrath may burn hot against them and I may consume them, in order that I may make a great nation of you.'"[7]

In other words, the Lord was planning to destroy the Israelites because of their disobedience to him. Yet Moses intervened, in essence asking God to have a change of heart. "But Moses implored the Lord his God and said, 'O Lord, why does your wrath burn hot against your people, whom you have brought out of the land of Egypt with great power and with a mighty hand?' Why should the Egyptians say, 'With evil intent did he bring them out, to kill them in the mountains and to consume them from the face of the earth'? Turn from your burning anger and relent from this disaster against your people."[8]

---

[7] Exodus 32:9-10 (ESV)
[7] Exodus 32:11-12 (ESV)

It worked. "And the Lord relented from the disaster that he had spoken of bringing on his people."[9]

Moses changed God's mind!

And God's mind was changed again in the third chapter of Jonah. The Lord told Jonah, "Arise, go to Nineveh, that great city, and call out against it the message that I tell you."[10] The message given to Jonah to give to the people, in a nutshell, was repent or else. "Jonah began to go into the city, going a day's journey. And he called out, 'Yet forty days, and Nineveh shall be overthrown!'"[11] But the people's hearts were changed. "And the people of Nineveh believed God. They called for a fast and put on sackcloth, from the greatest of them to the least of them."[12]

The Ninevites repented of their ways because of God's message through Jonah. "When God saw what they did, how they turned from their evil way, God relented of the disaster that he had said he would do to them, and he did not do it."[13]

Later, the Israelites were in trouble again. " . . . they provoked the Lord to anger with their deeds, and a plague broke out among them."[14]

However, someone changed God's mind. "Then Phinehas stood up and intervened, and the plague was stayed."[15]

---

[9] Exodus 32:14 (ESV)

[10] Jonah 3:2 (ESV)

[11] Jonah 3:4 (ESV)

[12] Jonah 3:5 (ESV)

[13] Jonah 3:10 (ESV)

[14] Psalm 106:29 (ESV)

[15] Psalm 106:30 (ESV)

In every case, God changed his mind because of people's actions.

Mary didn't fully comprehend the Son of God and his ultimate mission on earth, but she knew her son. And she wasn't afraid to go to him with a request.

Like Sand

When our son was diagnosed with autism, my husband and I were grappling with the daunting task of raising a child we were told would probably never speak and who would most likely have to be institutionalized. During this time, our pastor delivered a sermon that gave us hope.

He illustrated a point by explaining that those in Christ are like the sand on the bottom of a fish tank. Our strengths are like the hills of the sand and our weaknesses are like the valleys of the sand, but the water on top of the sand is level. That water is like our faithful Lord. Where our weaknesses (the sand) are the shallowest, our Lord's presence (the water) is the deepest. "But he said to me, 'My grace is sufficient for you, for my power is made perfect in weakness.' Therefore I will boast all the more gladly of my weaknesses, so that the power of Christ may rest upon me."[16]

We don't have to fear the perceived weaknesses of our sons and daughters. God calls us to kneel and pray, asking for his grace to be on our families and for his power to be evident in our children's lives.

---

[16] 2 Corinthians 12:9 (ESV)

41

As I was pondering this biblical passage, thankful for the hope this concept brought to our family, I was reminded of the *many* weaknesses I myself possess. The tears flowed as I realized my God also covers *me* with his grace and his power to achieve what he has called me to do—in this case, raise, along with my husband, incredible, gifted, successful children who will make a difference in their part of the world. It's a big task. We cannot do it alone. Thank God his grace is sufficient.

Mary, the Mom

Mary, of course, was Jewish. I have known few full-blooded Jewish women in my life. Hollywood often portrays a stereotypical Jewish woman as demanding, bossy, highly emotional, family-oriented, and even downright pushy. I would have made a great Jewish mom.

Let's think of Mary in this context while at the wedding in Cana. Can you see her standing with one hand on her robe-draped hip, flailing her other hand as she emotionally proclaimed her stance, using her mother-knows-best look to punctuate her words? She would have been a sight!

Even though she wasn't in a private setting, she probably wouldn't have held back her words or emotions. The one-sided conversation probably would have gone something like this: "Jesus, you're thirty years old. I thought you were going to *do* something with your life! You hang around with your twelve friends, bring them to the house—I cook and clean for them all—and still nothing's been happening. When are you going to get out there and make a change in this town?"

This may have been Mary's response after Jesus declared, "Why do you involve me?" Regardless, she continued with her request. She wanted to solve the social problem at this wedding. Jesus had other events on his mind. He was going to reveal his true identity by performing miracles in his own timing.

Jesus didn't have to "go out there" to make a change. He started the change right where he was.

And his mother pushed him into it a little sooner than he originally planned.

What strengths do you have? Weaknesses?

Remember, our weaknesses don't matter. God fills in where we need his strength.

Go to him, quickly, and pray a 2 Corinthians 12:9 (ESV) prayer:

Your grace is sufficient for me, Lord, for your power is made perfect in weakness. Therefore, I will boast all the more gladly about my weaknesses, so that your power may rest on me.

4

Talking with God

My husband and I pray for our kids every day. We go through the list of five in chronological order. And now that they are all adults, we've been joyfully adding their spouses' and children's names to our list. Sometimes we go through our prayer list out of routine, speaking prayers of peace and health and purpose. Sometimes there's a special need or an urgent request that we prayerfully pursue.

Prayer can feel like a stuffy, formal petition.

But it doesn't need to be that way.

One day my husband was thinking about Justice's used car and its obviously high mileage and all of the rattling, barely functioning, broken pieces acquired during that accumulated mileage. At one point in our prayer time, for the very first time ever, he added, "We pray for (Justice's) car, that it will last as long as he and his wife need it." This was just out of the blue; neither our son nor his wife had voiced a request.

That evening our Justice called. Their car had quit on them that very day. Their mechanic told them it wasn't worth fixing.

I laughed pretty hard and told him Dad prayed earlier for that car to last for as long as they needed it to. Clearly, God felt they didn't need that particular car any longer.

We shared this funny story with our other kids.

A week later, while the Leader, his wife and kids were over for supper, our oldest son asked, "Hey, Dad? You didn't happen to pray for our dishwasher did you?" Their dishwasher had quit on them that week. We had a good laugh again. Prayers, and the sometimes humorous results of them, are part of our family story.

As in the case of Justice's car, sometimes we get an almost immediate answer to our prayers.

The miracle at the wedding in Cana wasn't instantaneous, but Mary got an answer pretty quickly. She had a discussion with her son, the Son of God. We, too, can have a discussion with the Son of God, but in our timeline, we don't go to a physical Jesus. Our position may be in a church pew, our bedroom, our car, the bathroom floor, or wherever we're at.

What is it that brings us to our knees?

A friend of mine shared she shed many tears praying for her daughter. She said finally it came down to her telling God that she, as her mom, was giving up. In a sense she gave her daughter up to God because she didn't know what else to do. She said there certainly were no quick answers to her prayer. And, in fact, her daughter's situation went from bad to worse.

But God never let go of her daughter.

Slowly. Gradually. Her daughter started making different choices.

My friend says she is sometimes still amazed at where her daughter is today compared to ten years ago. She said, "I guess that's why we call it 'amazing grace.'"

Amazing grace.

One writer, Edward F. Markquart, shares his interpretation of the wedding at Cana this way: "I remember (my pastor) telling me, 'Markquart, this wedding story is pure grace. Pure grace. There is not one trace of judgment in the story. There are no put-downs such as 'you drink too much,' or 'you party too much.' This story is pure grace.'"[17]

And that's how Jesus receives us when we come to him in prayer.

No put-downs. No judgments.

Just pure, amazing grace.

At times I've felt shame and guilt as I come to my Lord in prayer, feeling as if I've perhaps contributed or caused the very problems that I'm now coming to him for, crying out for sweet relief.

But those are my own feelings to deal with.

He's never chastised me when I come to him with a need.

We pray because whatever is happening in our life at that time, we want something different. We

[17] "180 Gallons of Grace," Edward F. Markquart, sermonsfromseattle.com

pray because we desire different health, different happiness, different happenstance than what we have in that moment. We want to ease or improve our situation in life.

If we are living in righteousness, when those needs arise, we can have confidence that positive results will occur through our prayers.

"For the eyes of the Lord are on the righteous, and his ears are open to their prayer."[18]

Simply put, righteousness means blamelessness. We can't live blameless of our own accord. It's just not possible. We are human beings, and humans are born sinful. We need help to be blameless.

There is one thing that has hampered my prayers at times: my own sin—that thing that separates us from God. I struggle with selfishness and lack of empathy. I don't always take care of myself as I should. Of course, there's a multitude of other sins, but I won't bore you with the long list. These sometimes get in the way of our prayers. Sin truly does separate us from God. When I recognize this separation has occurred again, I repent. Surely, if I can't find the need to do it for myself, I can do it for the kids I am raising. Because the results of our sins never just fall back on us, they also fall back on those closest to us.

Make them bear their guilt, O God;
let them fall by their own counsels;
because of the abundance of their transgressions
cast them out,
for they have rebelled against you.

---

[18] 1 Peter 3:12 (ESV)

> But let all who take refuge in you rejoice;
> let them ever sing for joy,
> and spread your protection over them,
> that those who love your name may exult in you.
> For you bless the righteous, O Lord;
> you cover him with favor as with a shield.[19]

Without his forgiveness, our sin impedes our prayers.

With forgiveness, we are in a whole, new, clean standing with God.

Covered with his undeserved forgiveness, we're in a position to ask for our prayers to be answered.

We need Jesus.

We state our problems in the form of impassioned pleas, and sometimes we do it with a fist in the air, but don't stop there. Too many of us, in our spiritual infancy, pray and then expect the miracle to supernaturally happen. It *can* work that way. But I don't think it's the common way. After we pray, if we truly want something different to happen, we can't wait idly for the miracle to occur.

What we need to be doing when we experience a problem is, first, pray, and second, listen.

What we sometimes forget in the process of praying is that prayer is a two-way conversation. I originally titled this chapter "Talking to God," but then realized that's incorrect. We need to talk *with* God. Successful prayer is a conversation, not a list of wishes and wants submitted to an all-powerful benevolent one. As in all good relationships, there is a time to talk and a time to listen. If we are doing all

---

[19] Psalm 5:10-12 (ESV)

the talking and none of the listening, we are missing out on a huge benefit of prayer.

"Let the wise hear and increase in learning, and the one who understands obtain guidance ... "[20]

Years ago, as I read *Celebration of Discipline*, the author, Richard J. Foster, taught me how to listen after I prayed. The first morning after reading this, I was practicing my listening, sitting in my usual corner spot in the living room in my comfy chair. I had shut off the music I usually had on to drown out the cacophony of noise from five kids. I was sitting, intent on listening to what God had for me that morning, when a strange sound that I had never heard before came from *behind* me in the corner, directly in back of my chair. I quickly swiveled my chair to investigate what could possibly be making the noise, and discovered the large philodendron plant I had in the corner behind my chair was unfurling a beautiful brand new yellowish green leaf. I turned around just in time to see the completion of the new leaf opening. I had never witnessed such a wonder before.

I didn't know leaves made noise when they unfurled.

This, I learned, on my first day of being quiet.

This was not a coincidence. I believe the Lord timed the sound, timed the unfurling, however diminutive it was, to coincide with my new discipline. He was teaching me.

What else was I missing?

---

[20] Proverbs 1:5 (ESV)

It was a vivid "ah-ha" moment for me. I needed to practice listening to God after praying. God had revealed to me in that moment that I was missing a lot of beautiful things when I didn't stop and listen to him.

As I practiced and learned this skill, I realized I wasn't always the best at hearing him. Sometimes my own feelings and thoughts got in the way. But I also learned, he *always* heard me, even when my feelings weren't matching up with that truth.

And there's one more step to this prayer cycle.

We can't just listen to what God is saying to us, either. We also need to obey.

Remember Mary's advice: "Do whatever he tells you."[21]

Some scholars have suggested this is one of the most important verses in the Bible. It's pretty self-explanatory: do whatever he tells you. If you want true results from your prayers, you need to participate in the miracle—to do what God is telling you to do.

When we obey and do what God is telling us to do, then we're joining in his plan for our kids, our families, our futures. Our Heavenly Father knows what needs to be done.

Pray . . . Listen . . . Obey.

What would have once, in Mary's day, been a face-to-face discussion is now considered heart-to-ear prayer, from our hearts to God's ears:

> Give ear to my words, O Lord;
> consider my groaning.

---

[21] John 2:5b (ESV)

> Give attention to the sound of my cry,
>   my King and my God,
>   for to you do I pray.[22]

The dictionary describes prayer as a devout petition to God or an object of worship.[23]

There's a huge amount of material available on prayer. And, quite frankly, I'm not qualified to teach on all of those aspects.

I can, however, tell you about what happened in our family's story through prayer.

Miracles happened.

That's what happens when you go to Jesus.

Perhaps it's comforting for you to know that I didn't need to have a degree or get special training to learn how to pray. What I *did* need was to want something different for my kids badly enough to do something about it. I had plenty of on-the-job training!

And we didn't just pray once and wait. There was a high degree of persistence that occurred.

I'm not the only mom who has persisted in prayer:

> And he told them a parable to the effect that they ought always to pray and not lose heart. He said, "In a certain city there was a judge who neither feared God nor respected man. And there was a widow in that city who kept

---

[22] Psalm 5:1-2 (ESV)
[23] Dictionary.com

coming to him and saying, 'Give me justice against my adversary.' For a while he refused, but afterward he said to himself, 'Though I neither fear God nor respect man, yet because this widow keeps bothering me, I will give her justice, so that she will not beat me down by her continual coming.'" And the Lord said, "Hear what the unrighteous judge says. And will not God give justice to his elect, who cry to him day and night? Will he delay long over them? I tell you, he will give justice to them speedily. Nevertheless, when the Son of Man comes, will he find faith on earth?"[24]

One preacher puts it: "Ask, (and keep asking) and it will be given you."[25]

Persistence. Tenacity. Determination. Doggedness. Yes, even stubbornness.

Pursuing a miracle for our kids doesn't come easy.

But it's so worth it.

Author Mark Batterson writes: "Prayer turns ordinary parents into prophets who shape the destinies of their children, grandchildren, and every generation that follows."[26]

We're changing our kids' worlds! This is exciting!

---

[24] Luke 18:1-8 (ESV)
[25] gluthermonson.blogspot.com/2016/10/weary-faith
[26] Mark Batterson, *Praying Circles Around Your Children* (Grand Rapids: Zondervan, 2012), p. 11.

My husband and I won't quit praying for our kids until we die.

" . . . so our eyes look to the Lord our God, till he has mercy upon us."[27]

If we have breath left, my husband and I will still be praying, still bothering the Lord on behalf of our kids!

Parents' prayers pave the way to miracles.

Parents' prayers pave the way to miracles.

#SomeMiraclesNeedAMom | #AuthorSMcKeown

Mark Batterson agrees: "Prayer is . . . the difference between letting things happen and making things happen."[28] In the last chapter, when our daughter and her best friend were making plans with their boyfriends, we could have just "let things happen" and not said anything—and not prayed. But we did more. We prayed, asking for the Lord to help them make wise decisions. Did God send the *threat* of rain to help our daughter and her friends make the right decision? I believe he did.

We didn't want to just let things happen with our kids. Perceived outcomes for several of our kids were

---

[27] Psalm 123:2c (ESV)

[28] Mark Batterson, *Praying Circles Around Your Children* (Grand Rapids: Zondervan, 2012), p. 39.

not good when they were younger. If there was any chance those perceived outcomes could be different, we weren't afraid to fight for them—while on our knees.

When we stop, get to our knees and pray, our reach is extended beyond our immediate home.

#SomeMiraclesNeedAMom | #AuthorSMcKeown

As a praying mom, I also learned to dress my kids in the Armor of God through prayer, especially if they were going through a rough time or would be away from my immediate reach. Some single moms raising challenging children have asked my recommendation for equipping their child to stay at their dad's home for the weekend. They didn't like some of the influences around their children when they were away.

I reminded them that they can't be with their kids at all times; but God can. I also encouraged them as they hugged their kids goodbye for the weekend to dress their kids in the Armor of God. "For we do not wrestle against flesh and blood, but against the rulers, against the authorities, against the cosmic powers over this present darkness, against the spiritual forces of evil in the heavenly places."[29] (Yes,

---

[29] Ephesians 6:12 (ESV)

that sometimes includes exes). But as much as we can be mistaken in our thinking that it is our fellow man that is our enemy, it is not. When we pray for our kids to have the helmet of salvation on their head, the belt of truth about their waist, the breastplate of righteousness on their chest, the gospel of peace on their feet, the shield of faith in one hand, and the sword of the spirit in the other, they are dressed for going out into the world and away from a mom that can't be with them every step of the way. They are spiritually protected.

In *The Armor of God*, Priscilla Shirer writes that we pray, "So that the enemy will know beyond any reasonable doubt that his number is up and his game is done."[30]

Oh, how I wish I'd learned this sooner!

When commanders prepare for war, they make strategic plans to ensure the best possible outcome. When we appeal with strategic prayers for our kids, we are increasing a positive outcome for them. That's the goal. That's the fight. That's where the rubber meets the road. When we pray, we help our kids achieve the best possible outcome.

It takes time to learn to pray, and trust, when life isn't going as planned, but we can take the lessons we learn and pass them on to others. My husband works for the railroad industry, in which all work positions are based on seniority. New hires, usually the younger ones, are the first to be furloughed during downturns

---

[30] Priscilla Shirer, *The Armor of God* (Nashville: Lifeway, 2015), p. 5.

in the economy. And, due to the railroad being closely tied to farming and manufacturing, my husband was often furloughed for at least a couple of months in the first part of the year during the early years of our marriage.

One time the economy was especially unstable, which created extra financial challenges for our family. I am the family bookkeeper, so I was the one that paid the bills. Dismayed, at one point I realized we had a mere ten dollars left to feed our family of four (at that stage of our life) for two weeks.

What to do?

I went to my Lord.

I prayed.

I read his Word.

And then I listened.

I had prayed, telling him (as if he didn't know) that ten dollars wouldn't go far in the grocery store, then asking him to multiply that last ten dollars so my husband and I could feed our babies. I believed he told me that *he* was the best investment possible.

So, if he was the best investment, I figured I should give *him* one hundred percent of what I had. It wasn't hard to count!

And I trusted my Lord.

A few days later, on a Sunday morning, I prayed, "Lord, I believe I've heard from you that I need to trust you and act on this trust. Here is our last ten dollars. I'm trusting you for whatever you decide is best for the outcome."

I placed that wrinkled ten dollar bill in the offering plate and watched it pass all the way down to the end of the pew and into the usher's hands. The decision was done.

And then I listened to the sermon, picked up my kids from children's church, and walked with my husband to the car.

Once we got in the car, my husband, quite excitedly, said, "Someone in church (we barely knew this man) came to me and said he was feeling he was supposed to give us $125. Here's the check!"

We had an answer immediately! We were so excited!! God answered my prayers! And I bought food for my babies that week!

Have you ever had *your* prayers answered? If not, let me remind you of this quote from Winston Churchill, a man that experienced success, failure, and led his country through a very tumultuous time in history. He said, "Success is going from failure to failure without losing enthusiasm."[31]

Don't give up on prayer even if you've had failures in this area. There are reasons we don't get answers to our prayers that we won't ever be able to understand. The steps here in this chapter are things you *can* do to fight for something different for your kids.

Trust him.

Do you pray for your kids every day?

If not, what can you do to remember to do that?

---

[31] *101 Motivating Quotes on Success*, positivityblog.com, Winston Churchill

Have you been discouraged by your answers to prayer in the past?

Can you see past the discouragement? If not, I encourage you to go to a wise friend or pastor to help you if you're stuck in that discouragement.

In the meantime, pray this simple prayer: *Dear Lord, help me not to grow faint or be discouraged!*[32]

---

[32] Isaiah 42:4a (ESV)

5

Do Whatever He Tells You

Mary turned to the servants and said, "Do whatever he tells you."[33]

Why would she say that? What was she thinking? What were the *servants* thinking? First of all, I believe Mary was done making her stance with her son. She'd said her piece. Her discussion with Jesus was over on this topic. It was now time for action.

Second, she had a close relationship with him. She had a better understanding than her typical neighbor down the dirt path of what simple obedience meant. After all, she had lived with the Son of God. His daily presence, before he began traveling, changed her worldview. She learned, after kneeling and praying, asking for direction and guidance, to stand and "do."

---

[33] John 2:5 (ESV)

61

But how do we know what is it we're supposed to *do*?

Whatever

How do we figure out the "whatever" part in the *do whatever he tells you* directive?

Proverbs has a hint:

> To know wisdom and instruction, *to understand words of insight, to receive instruction in wise dealing,* (italics mine) in righteousness, justice, and equity; *to give prudence to the simple, knowledge and discretion to the youth* (italics mines)—Let the wise hear and increase in learning, and the one who understands obtain guidance, to understand a proverb and a saying, the words of the wise and their riddles. The fear of the Lord is the beginning of knowledge; fools despise wisdom and instruction.[34]

To understand words of insight and to receive instruction when we desperately need it means we "hear and increase in learning."[35] "It includes skill in living—following God's design and thus avoiding moral pitfalls."[36] Reading the Word is one step of

---

[34] Proverbs 1:2-7 (ESV)
[35] Proverbs 1:5a (ESV)
[36] Proverbs 1:2 Study Notes (*The New International Study Bible*); Kenneth Barker, General Editor (Grand Rapids: Zondervan, 1995).

many in developing the skill of listening so you understand what you're supposed to be doing.

I've heard of toddlers getting away from their mothers and crawling a mile away, miraculously making it safely across busy roads and ending up among strangers. In today's world, we certainly know why this is a dangerous occurrence. But how do we know, as adults, that what we are doing is right? How do we know when we're going the wrong direction? Again, those verses in Proverbs mention fear of the Lord.[37] It's "a loving reverence for God that includes submission to his lordship and to the commands of his word."[38] If our understanding of God and his directives don't change as we grow older, we can get stuck in a spiritual infancy that hinders our life's journey.

Sometimes we just hear wrong, or we don't listen to the entire message. I've certainly done that.

I was prepping for my annual guests one summer: a car full of women from Iowa arriving to talk, walk, and shop for three days. We bonded during the parenting years, in adjoining foxholes during the "parenting war." We would slip each other intel; often, something as simple as, "Yeah, that didn't work for me, either." That bond carried us through to our "empty nest" phase, which we now celebrate with great enthusiasm.

---

[37] Proverbs 1:7a (ESV)
[38] Proverbs 1:7 Study Notes (The New International Study Bible); Kenneth Barker, General Editor (Grand Rapids: Zondervan, 1995).

My husband had left the day before to go to his brother's cabin for the duration of the gals' visit. After he left, though, I realized I would be alone overnight for the first time in our new house. I had to think through the process: "What do you do when staying alone?" I answered myself (aren't I clever): "Lock all the doors." So, I did.

Afterwards, I noticed we had a full magazine basket. (I was still making sure all was ready for my guests). I decided to thin this out. But rather than taking the old magazines to the garage at night, I placed the pile on the kitchen counter to take them out first thing in the morning.

And that's what I did. On my way to make coffee that next morning, I saw the stack of magazines and immediately took the pile and placed it in the recycle bin, turned around to go back into the house, and . . . I. Could not. Get in. The door was locked. Evidently, I had locked the handle rather than the deadbolt. The handle had released and allowed me to go out, but it wouldn't allow me back into the house.

I was stuck in the garage, without a key, without a phone, and without proper clothing. (It was July! I had worn appropriate clothing for bed, but it just wouldn't cut it out in the neighborhood!)

Desperate for a solution, I began walking around the garage, searching. I spotted my husband's overalls, which he wears while crawling under his cars. I spent about three seconds eyeballing that lovely garment. It was oily, filthy, and smelled, and let's be honest: it would have been a herculean struggle to get my husband's size "L" on my XL "robust" frame.

So . . . I kept looking . . . and searching . . . and I came up with . . . nothing. Nada. Zilch. What to do?

I sat down and prayed.

"Lord, I'm stuck. I need your help. The ladies are arriving in just a few hours, and it's really hot out here. I would prefer to shower and have clothes on before they arrive. Do you have any ideas for me?"

For me, this process of seeking an answer involves praying, focusing on God, and hearing with my heart what comes next.

I heard from him directly! I *swear* I heard the word "sledgehammer."

Immediately, I jumped up and said, "Ooh! Great idea, Lord!"

I knew where the sledgehammer was, so I went right to work. I had to swing it several times before the handle gave way, but it eventually did. The handle eventually dangled . . . and it was a beautiful sight.

Finally, I could go about the business of the day!

After the ladies arrived, we had a good laugh about my predicament and subsequent resolution. We had our three days of fun, the ladies left, and then I waited for my husband's return. Soon, I saw his car coming around the curve of our cul-de-sac and went out to the garage to greet him, blocking the still-dangling door handle. I wanted him to hear my reason for destroying the handle before he saw it and jumped to horrible (and surely inaccurate) conclusions.

But he was walking too fast.

I tried to engage him in conversation. "Hi, honey! How was kayaking?" But he was answering my questions and walking at the same time. (Since when did my husband acquire the ability to multi-task?)

So . . . to get him to slow down, I changed my tone and abruptly declared, "I've got something to tell you."

He stopped walking immediately. Ah. This is what I wanted. (Evidently, after forty-plus years of marriage, I can still give him cause for concern!)

I explained what had happened and how I believe God told me "sledgehammer."

With a pained look, he responded, "I wish you had listened a little bit longer. I keep the key right next to the sledgehammer."

Sigh.

I was *so* close.

But I jumped into action too soon. I didn't listen for the entire direction. Was he trying to tell me the key was *next to* the sledgehammer? Or was he helping me learn how I too often use a big tool unnecessarily, bullying my way through, when all I really need is a tiny key to get where I need to be?

Oh, Lord, help me to hear you better!

How can we get better at hearing from our Lord that "whatever" that he wants us to do, if we don't truly listen? To get better at hearing, I believe, we need to practice, practice, practice.

The Hard Part

There's always a hard part.

Author Mark Batterson writes, "We don't really stop to think about what life on the ark was like, but I think it's safe to say that Noah didn't get much sleep.

He was feeding, cleaning, and caring for thousands of animals around the clock. And it must have smelled to high heaven. Did you know that African elephants produce eighty pounds of waste per day? It was smelly and messy. And that's a pretty accurate picture of what obedience looks like. Obedience is hard work, and it gets harder."[39]

The picture Batterson describes can certainly be used to describe what moms do daily: *feeding, cleaning, and caring for children around the clock.* It *is* hard work. And like he mentions, it's often smelly and messy, and sleep is limited. Hard work is required. We don't stand back, do nothing, and say, "I declare this miracle to occur." We don't (can't) say, "I declare for my children to be highly functioning, future upstanding, successful members of the United States of America." It won't just happen by verbally declaring it! Raising children doesn't work that way.

If we want a miracle for our kids, hard work is required.

#SomeMiraclesNeedAMom | #AuthorSMcKeown

---

[39] Mark Batterson, *All In* (Grand Rapids: Zondervan, 2013), p. 101.

Understand

My husband is from a naturally sarcastic family. Sarcasm doesn't work for every family, I know, but it did for his. So he and I often used sarcasm as a way to teach *our* children. Getting Determined to eat was often a battle. Coaxing with words and pouring more ketchup on top of his food didn't always work, so we reverted to sarcasm. It went something like, "I'll bet you can't take another bite!" After which he would often cheerfully take another bite. One day, while at the dinner table, I *didn't* want Determined to take another bite. (I believe I needed to give him a spoonful of medicine first). After I said, "Don't take a bite," my son's blue eyes sparkled with mischief, thinking he'd just heard another line of sarcasm, and quickly took a bite. My husband read my face immediately, which was full of unbelief that my son had just totally disobeyed me, and he quickly explained the irony of the situation in defense of our son. My maternal, emotional reaction to my son's supposed disobedience was immediate. I was shocked that my son would disobey my request. Of course, he was only misunderstanding the intent of my words. But when we know what we're supposed to do and don't do it, I wonder at the hurt we inflict on our Lord. We are withholding from him the language of his love. Obedience is not always easy!

At the wedding in Cana, Jesus didn't just declare for the miracle to happen. He could have simply made the wine appear. He could have said a few words, or just nodded, or done nothing at all but willed it to be. He certainly had the power to do so! But instead, work and obedience was required . . . and Mary led the way. She saw that it was possible; she knew that work was required.

More Work

I mentioned earlier that when our youngest son was first diagnosed with autism, we chose not to follow all professional recommendations. Against initial suggestions, we kept him at home. My social worker friend pointed out to me pretty passionately (and rightly) how full my plate already was. Why add more? But my husband and I felt it was best for our son to keep him at home. And that involved a lot of work.

A new neighbor moved in down the street, and we met and visited for a while as our kids played in my front yard. She was an occupational therapist with Easter Seals. I explained to her our son's new diagnosis and told her that he only qualified for hands-on physical therapy once a month through the local education system. This new friend went right to work teaching me what I should be doing for our son.

Through the combined teaching of our new neighbor and a pre-school educational professional, I developed a morning schedule. This son and I played with a blanket; we rolled him up in it and held him tight while he was in it. We would play with "gak," a slimy, gooey substance that I detested, but he needed to play with it. We would spray shaving cream on a cookie sheet and play and write in it. We would fill a baby bathtub with dry rice and cotton balls, and coax him to sit in it with only his diaper on to teach him how to experience the varied textures. We took pictures of his favorite items around the house, labeled the pictures, and used them as flashcards to help him put words to common household items.

These things took time and work. I was a mother of four married to a traveling man. This was not easy. But I felt I was doing what I was supposed to be doing. And I didn't always get everything else done like I wanted to. Dirty laundry and dirty dishes piled up; groceries were bought when they absolutely had to be. The quality of my "homemaking" slumped to a new low while I honed in on therapy for my son. Did it make life easier for us? On the contrary. It made life more chaotic, more difficult, and more stressful. But we chose it. This is something we felt compelled to do to pursue a different future for our son than what had been predicted.

One of my sisters-in-law, from whom I learned so much about parenting, was also known amongst the family for her lack of housekeeping skills. It didn't matter to her, because her *kids* are what mattered to her. Whether you tend to be more like June Cleaver, who vacuums while wearing a pearl necklace, or more like Roseanne Conner, someone who is just struggling to get her dysfunctional family through the day, my sister-in-law had a home where family was very important. And it was a home we loved hanging out in.

One day when my traveling man came home after being gone for three days, he stepped through the front door, looked around the living room and dining room of our house, saw a new level of inconceivable mess, and said, "Debbie'd be proud." To be fair, the house did look like I hadn't picked up anything during all the days he had been gone—and I probably hadn't. It had been a particularly difficult few days with the kids, and my patience level was shot, so my reaction to my husband's words were swift, "Look! Your kids are *alive*! That's all I could accomplish these last few days!"

My husband quietly set his grip (a railroader's duffle) down in the entryway, started rolling up his sleeves, and began picking up.

A New Faith

According to Hebrews, "Now faith is the assurance of things hoped for, the conviction of things not seen."[40]

Moms and dads, grandparents and caretakers, you can be commended, too, when you are *sure* of what you hope for and *certain* of what you do not see. It is a faith that those who haven't walked in your Nikes have little understanding about.

When a physician told us that our fourth son would never speak and would most likely need to be institutionalized, fear was my first reaction. I feared for our son's future, I feared that we would have a child who did not function well on a daily basis, and I feared he would need constant care well into our waning years. Faith, for us, was a decision.

---

[40] Hebrews 11:1 (ESV)

I shared before how I implemented the "shoes system" to communicate with this son where he was going so he wouldn't have a tantrum in public. When he began kicking and screaming at home rather than at church, my hope for our son roared to life. I understood for the first time that he wasn't limited in his capacity to think, he was limited in his capacity to *communicate*. There was a big difference! I had faith for the first time that he could accomplish much if I could help him understand the world around him. My faith for my son's future was renewed. My faith, in that instance, was built on the obedience I had put into action, carefully putting select shoes on my son to communicate with him.

But there was a lot more work to be done.

I needed to keep track of all those shoes to keep our fragile line of communication clear.

I also needed to work with him daily on the sensory issues that caused him to scream whenever he came across something that disturbed his comfort zone, such as water, Styrofoam, or food that he chose based on texture rather than taste.

I did all of this because I believed. I had faith he had a promising future.

Remember, I didn't fabricate this faith out of thin air. I prayed a little prayer: "Help me, Lord." I was praying for wisdom in how to communicate with my son, but God gave me so much more: faith for our circumstances.

Which leads to another element the servants at Cana used that day: trust.

Total Trust

Proverbs promises, "Trust in the Lord with all your heart, and do not lean your own understanding. In all your ways acknowledge him, and he will make straight your paths."[41]

Servants are naturally submissive. They are paid to be so. "Jesus said to the servants, "Fill the jars with water."[42] It doesn't discuss how much work the servants needed to do. First, gather the water; second, fill the jars. Remember, the house was full of guests. The servants would have been busy with numerous other tasks keeping everyone comfortable. Jesus had just added to their list of what needed to be done. Can you relate, moms?

Some scholars tell us that water was collected from rooftops, or streams, or a public well of some kind. There were no convenient faucets. But, regardless, there was work to be done to simply "fill the jars with water."

We don't understand why we have to go through the things we do to accomplish a task. We don't understand why we don't always have compliant children who learn easily and soar to heights unimagined, seemingly without any difficulties at all. It is the life we live. God knows this isn't easy. There is a reason we have children who have challenges. God knows why. *We* can't always know why.

The attributes of obedience, hard work, faith, and trust intertwine. We need to just start with one of

---

[41] Proverbs 3:5-6 (ESV)
[42] John 2:7 (ESV)

them, making sure we're going in the right direction, of course.

The writer of the Gospel of John portrays Mary as someone who trusts her son and whatever he says. She knew him. She understood him. She trusted him.

If we keep God at a distance, is it a wonder we don't trust him as we should?

The servants mentioned in these verses were most likely paid to do whatever they were told to do. They didn't know why they were filling those jars full of water. They were just doing what they were told to do.

Mary, on the other hand, was trusting that Jesus knew what he was talking about. In the privacy of their home years earlier, did Jesus instruct Mary to complete a simple task and the outcome was a miracle? I believe this could have happened because the result was here at the wedding she was so full of faith. She fully trusted in Jesus, who trusted the servants would obey. Trust was part of the equation of this miracle.

Years ago, my family was on vacation and we made a stop at an aunt and uncle's home. We were all gathered in the family room when I looked over at my brother, who was reading a book. The title read, *How to Live Like a King's Kid*, written by Harold Hill. I naively thought to myself, "How in the world can a kid get his father to become as rich as a king?" I certainly liked my dad—I didn't want a different one—but I approached my brother, asking him to let me read the book when he was finished with it.

My brother gave it to me and once we were back at home I went to my room and read it from cover to cover and prayed for a personal relationship with Jesus Christ. I had been attending church on Sundays with my family, but that attendance had no effect on my life Monday through Saturday. This prayer was the start of a fresh awareness for me.

Have you taken ahold of that fresh awareness? It can be yours if you ask.

Mark writes, "For whoever does the will of God, he is my brother and sister and mother."[43]

Are you ready to do whatever God is asking of you?

What is the Lord asking you to do today?

Do you know? If not, have you prayed for Him to show you?

A simple prayer: *Lord, please show me what you want me to do next. And give me the strength to do it.*

---

[43] Mark 3:35 (ESV)

6

Sometimes You Do It Afraid

Sometimes you end up needing to do things for your family you really don't want to do. And sometimes there's risk involved. It's called "doing it afraid."

Four boys plus seven years and then . . . unexpectedly . . . our only girl. This equation, along with a father/daughter duo that is very close creates a challenging scenario for any guy trying to marry our girl.

But there was this guy that was up for the challenge. (Note: this is a different guy than the one mentioned in chapter three).

We've taught all five of our kids that marriage is forever, so there are some parameters they need to keep in mind. We are practicing Christians, of course, so faith was one of the "must haves" we stressed. We taught our kids if they had that foundation, their marriage would be off to a great start.

Our daughter dated this guy for approximately one and a half years. He had the foundational requirement but several of us in the family were getting concerned. He was a band member in a start-up band that didn't have "full-time" status. All of the other members of this band had dependable secondary part-time jobs to support them as they pursued their dreams with the band. Not our daughter's boyfriend. We had conversations about it—with both our daughter and her boyfriend—but nothing changed. This mid-twenty-something was working only when gigs were scheduled, needed parental financial assistance often, and had no foreseeable plans to change his situation.

I liked this guy! He was a nice kid. He seemed to care for our daughter, but the fact that he wouldn't "adult" when he needed to was concerning.

One day I brought it up with my husband. "I think it's time we say something about this guy."

My husband's response surprised me. "I can't, Sandy! If she cuts us off like our Wanderer did and never talks to us again, it'll kill me." We had been estranged from our Wanderer for several years. The mere thought of it occurring with another one of our kids bumped against deep wounds.

We were driving in the car while having this conversation, so I didn't have any place to go except wherever he drove us. When you're a passenger on a journey and you don't like how the journey is going, what are your options? We rode in heavy silence as I contemplated what to do next.

Years ago, when the Conductor and I decided it was time to purchase the first family computer, it took us two years to agree on which one to purchase! I didn't have the luxury of two years in this situation. In a perfect world, my husband and I would have blissfully agreed without any difficulty and walked together, hand-in-hand, toward a solution. But that's not the way it always worked in our family. Real families don't always function "by the book."

Deciding the best option was to pray, I asked the Lord to give me direction. If the Lord said to leave it alone, so be it. If he said I should speak up, I would be going solo on this endeavor. This had become totally clear. I understood my husband's fear, but I also remembered our friend's advice so many years before: "You don't make decisions based on fear. You make decisions based on whether it's right or not."

So, I prayed.

I waited.

And I did a little research.

Fear doesn't belong in family decision-making.

#SomeMiraclesNeedAMom | #AuthorSMcKeown

I am an avid follower of author Gary Thomas' blog. My husband and I have used much of the material in his books and his blogs in our volunteer roles as marriage mentors and pre-marriage teachers in a church setting. I pulled up all of Gary's blogs on my computer and re-read the ones that discussed choosing a mate. After reading them all—which included years of knowledge from a much smarter guy than myself—I felt quite certain I was on the correct path. Something needed to be said. I became even more convinced of this when a woman I was mentoring at the time confirmed it for me. In one of our weekly meetings, she asked how I was doing, and I shared what I was praying about—whether to challenge our daughter to break it off with her boyfriend or not. And this woman I was mentoring said, "I wish someone had said something to me. Life would have been so much easier if I had married a man that walked with God."

A couple of weeks later, as I was praying and reminding the Lord I was still waiting for an answer, he responded. I felt I was given a step-by-step process to walk through with my daughter. *But I didn't share this with my husband.* There were two reasons why. One, my husband would have surely tried to talk me out of it; and two, in the off-chance it did go sour, I needed him to be an innocent bystander.

I needed to wait a little longer for my plan to begin, though. But, one day, the question I was waiting for from my husband finally came: "What do you want to do for your birthday?"

My birthday was a little more than a week away at the time and it landed on a Saturday. He thought I would want to do something big to celebrate, but I had another idea.

"I'd like to go out to breakfast with our daughter and her boyfriend," I announced.

He wrinkled his forehead. "Really?"

I assured him that was what I wanted: "It is *my* birthday." Giving up one more thing as a mom— my birthday and what I *really* wanted to do to celebrate—would be a very small price to pay in the long run. Remember, we need to parent with an eternal mindset.

So I texted our daughter and asked her if she could check with her boyfriend and see if they could join us for breakfast to celebrate. She got back to me later and confirmed they were available. The location and time were set.

Now, hear me. I wanted to meet for breakfast partly because there was a recent incident between the boyfriend and one of my husband's extended family members that left some relatives incredulous. I won't go into it in detail, but the number of people that were questioning our daughter dating this guy was multiplying rapidly. However, I had only *heard* about what occurred. I did not see what had happened, nor had I heard the boyfriend's perspective. My plan was to ask about the incident at some point during the breakfast. If he confirmed the previously reported facts, I planned to find a way to discuss this with our daughter alone. If he was, in fact, innocent of what I had heard, I planned on letting the matter drop.

We were seated in a very busy restaurant. Everyone ordered and we caught up about our weeks since we last saw each other. I then casually asked our daughter's boyfriend what had happened. And he relayed what had happened *exactly* how I had heard it. He was not embarrassed at all. (Although the entire family thought he should be!) I listened, and then I changed the subject. Unbeknownst to anyone else at the table, my decision was made.

At the end of the breakfast I asked my daughter if she wanted to help me use some birthday coupons shopping at a nearby department store—gifts are one of her love languages, so I was pretty sure she would say yes—and she didn't disappoint. We said goodbye to the guys, and she and I drove off to the mall. After parking the car, she started to open her door, and I stopped her.

"Just a minute. We need to talk about something," I started. And she, just like her father is apt to, lost color in her face at those words. That is almost the worst thing you can say to those two!

She timidly shut the car door.

I then began telling her what I had learned from author Gary Thomas: "Adam stood behind Eve and said nothing when she was about to make a poor choice. I can no longer say nothing."

And I relayed to her how, as a mentor to women, I have sat across the table from too many women whose husbands refused to work. And I continued, "Honey, if he won't work for you while you're dating, he won't work for you while you're married."

She responded, "I've been thinking about these things, but I thought I was overthinking them."

I assured her she was not.

And then she told me some other things that were bugging her about him that I didn't even know about.

I hid my shock to the best of my ability and then challenged, "It's time for this relationship to be done."

She reached for me and I held her there in the car in the parking lot of the mall while she sobbed.

Then, wiping her eyes, she announced she needed to talk to a couple of her girlfriends. I gave her privacy in the car and walked to a nearby bench—and prayed. I had forgotten my phone at home before we left for breakfast earlier. I didn't even have a human lifeline to call. It was just God and I on that bench. In that time I was praying, "Your will be done, Lord."

She came and found me after her phone calls, and we walked around the department store a little, but our hearts really weren't in it. We soon left and, as we were deciding where to go next, she said, "I don't know how to break this up, what do I do?"

I advised, "Let's go home and ask Dad. He's broken up with girls before, he'll know what to do!"

So we drove home and surprised my husband. He wasn't expecting both of us so soon in the afternoon—or the news we had to share. As our daughter told my husband she had decided to break up with her boyfriend, my husband's head snapped around—shocked—and looked at me with several questions in his eyes, but wisely saved those for later. He, instead, tended to his daughter, holding her in his arms and comforting her.

We talked for the next several hours. We were all exhausted from the emotional toll the conversation had taken and decided to take a break. Our daughter declared her stomach was complaining about missing lunch, and my husband promised he would get *anything* she wanted to eat. Our daughter chose the family staple: popcorn. We were eating the freshly popped corn when our oldest son and his two kids arrived to wish me a happy birthday. They found three emotionally exhausted people. But it was a turn for the better for our daughter.

One of my biggest fears in all of this was the advice our daughter would receive from her previous college roommate. Her roommate had married already and she and her husband double-dated with our daughter and her boyfriend often. They hung out together extensively. My fear was this friend would tell our daughter that we were overreacting and not to break up. But my fear was unfounded. My daughter reported this friend's response to me a few days later.

She said, "That relationship hasn't been working for months!"

Both my husband and I had fears that did not come to fruition in this case. I do not recommend moving forward with decisions without your spouse being in agreement with you, but fear was getting in the way for several of us in this example. It needed to be swiftly dealt with, and, I believe, the Lord directed me in how to do that.

When we obey, Jesus shows himself to us. What can go wrong when he's involved?

Fear is too often a part of family decisions. What "ifs" and "maybes" get in the way.

Bob Goff writes in *Everybody Always*, "People who are becoming love experience the same experiences we all do. They just stop letting fear call the shots."[44]

I couldn't have said it better.

What are *you* afraid of today?

Is there something you are feeling nudged to deal with but fear is stopping you?

A simple prayer: *Lord, I don't want to be stuck and afraid anymore. Please show me clearly how to move forward. Strengthen me and uphold me with your righteous hand.*

---

[44] Bob Goff, *Everybody Always* (Nashville: Nelson Books, 2018), p. 17.

7

Sometimes You Do It in Peace

I've received a few unexpected phone calls from my husband. They usually start like this:

"Hi. I'm in an ambulance on the way to the hospital."

And my response is usually, "Again?"

Most people experience a time in their life where they come to realize just how fragile life really is. My husband has had that pleasure repeatedly.

The Conductor is an avid cyclist—the ten-speed kind. At sixty-three years old, he averages forty miles a day during the warmer seasons of the Midwest. More time spent on the trail increases his chances of face-planting on those trails.

A few months ago, I received the most recent phone call. He was riding his bike to his sister's to help her with some things around the house, but ran into a moving car while he was looking in the other direction.

So I received a phone call, and I made a phone call, and that person made a phone call . . . and the emergency room in the hospital had enough people for a party!

As we were waiting for the results of x-rays, MRIs, and doctor consultations, we were joking around and having a great time. The attending nurse came back after completing one of her tasks down the hall and said, "The nurses on the other side of this door are loving the laughter. We don't hear that much down here!" Not long after that comment, a security guard stopped in the doorway: "It sounds like a party in here, there's a lot of laughing going on." I responded with my you-can-laugh-or-you-can-cry canned comment, but I was really feeling pretty calm.

The doctor eventually came in and announced that my husband, who had been lying in the bed during all this laughter and grimacing, "Please don't make me laugh!" had broken vertebrae, broken ribs, a partially collapsed lung, and a separated shoulder. The doctor announced, "We'll be keeping him for a few days." And I *still* was calm.

One of our daughters-in-law, a nurse, called and lamented California was too far for her to come immediately to help take care of him. She also warned that, at sixty-three, the medical staff might require my husband to move to an intermediate medical facility to recover from his significant injuries. I was still calm.

My husband's youngest sister called. She is married to an orthopedic surgeon. An offer was made for a second opinion, which we accepted gladly. And the peace continued.

The peace stayed with me . . . until I was home alone that night at 1:30 in the morning.

I was tossing and turning (not anything unusual for me in this menopausal season of my life), contemplating the events of the day. Rather than continuing to lie there, I decided to get out of bed and read my Bible. I settled in my favorite spot in the living room, picked up my Bible that I've owned for almost forty years, and turned immediately, without intent, to Isaiah 26:3. A friend had recently shared that particular verse with me, and I had highlighted it. My eyes fell on the words: *"You will keep in perfect peace him whose mind is steadfast, because he trusts in you."*

I felt like God was reassuring me directly.

Unfaltering. Resolute. Unswerving. Firm. And . . . at peace.

I knew the Lord had my husband and our future in his hands. I had no doubt of this. He was assuring me with his Word.

And he kept doing it. I had total confidence God had this.

As the days went on, we discovered my husband didn't need *any* physical therapy due to his excellent physical condition. (Yay!) And he got to come home after only three days in the hospital.

Of course, taking care of a patient 24/7 who is at your total mercy when you don't have the gift of mercy can bring a whole host of complications.

A friend who was an orthopedic nurse for four decades was texting prayers to my phone in between advice on how to take care of my husband. In one of the early texts, she sent a quick prayer: "And help Sandy to be kind."

Oh, how my friend knows and understands me! She also understood my husband and I both needed prayer.

A week after my husband was home, his boss stopped by for a visit. He informed us that my Conductor husband might be forced to retire if his back injuries were too severe and didn't heal well. He wanted us to be prepared for the possibility.

After his boss left, the Conductor and I talked it through. It wouldn't be our first choice for him to retire earlier than planned, but we knew we'd be fine.

A few weeks after my husband's bike accident, something else happened.

Our daughter, who was living with us in the transition time between college graduation and finding her first apartment, was having car troubles. The Conductor loves to tinker with cars, but was unable to do so while wearing an unyielding body brace. So, I told her she could use my car for the hour drive to work. I would use my electric bike to go to the gym and meet with my friend. Driving my new electric bike to the gym would be a fun, new experience, I was sure. Going *to* the gym wasn't the problem. Coming back afterwards was. I was on my way home when I came across gravel spilled on the shoulder of the road and didn't see it soon enough. With the speed of the bike cranked to 20 mph, I was too inexperienced to react. The front tire wobbled nastily, and I went down hard. I picked up the bike, and myself, and continued my journey home. I walked on that right ankle for a week before it swelled to the point I could no longer ignore something was wrong. A surgeon confirmed it was severely sprained with torn tendons on both sides.

What a duo my husband and I made! He in his body cast, me in my boot, alternating between crutches and a medical scooter. We weren't enjoying this season, but we were at peace. (Except when he beat me at cribbage!) It was a long summer. And we survived it.

Sometimes life's journeys have steep, uphill trails. We don't get to pick the seasons we're in. But we do get to pick what kind of approach and manner we will have going through those seasons.

Will we choose to rely on God and his comforting Word?

Or will we worry about all the shouldas and couldas, and wished we'd done it differently?

The story in the Gospel of John of the miracle at Cana doesn't tell us why this wedding became an unintentionally dry one. If neighbors failed to bring wine, as was the custom, why didn't they? Were the guests especially thirsty—possibly, as has been suggested, already inebriated? The master of ceremonies questioned the wisdom of bringing out the better wine as these guests wouldn't notice the difference.

We don't always get to know or understand why something happens that is not in our plans. But we can understand, and learn, how to get through those times with grace and dignity.

Sometimes we come across people that don't understand our peace.

I got a phone call from Justice's school counselor one day. She was dismayed to see that he had not ordered a commencement gown. She was calling to inquire why.

I told her, "This son has not enjoyed his time at your school. He does not see the merit of celebrating with his peers."

She pushed further, "I am concerned he will forever regret not walking with his classmates in his graduation ceremony."

I countered (irritated parent alert), "You don't know my son. And, in fact, I'm a little frustrated that this is the first time he's on your radar. He has gotten some low grades on his report card. He has been in the principal's office for conduct. He's been on an Individualized Educational Program (IEP) for reading. But the first time I hear from you is because he has failed to purchase a commencement gown."

She ignored my frustrations and pushed again, "If money is the issue, I will be happy to purchase the gown for him at my own expense."

I suppose I really should have thanked her for her offer and let it go, but I was still focused on her lack of understanding of my son, "Money. Is not. The issue."

And, finally, to end the conversation as amicably as possible, I offered, "If you would like to attempt to encourage him in this matter, go for it. But I don't think you're going to get anywhere with him, to be honest."

We said our niceties and hung up.

I never mentioned it to Justice. (We were barely speaking at the time, other than in counseling sessions). He never mentioned whether she pursued it with him. It wasn't a battle worth fighting. We were not trying to have a child who fit in with his peers, doing what they were all doing, to be part of "normal" society. We were fighting for our child to succeed in life! Could he succeed without walking the commencement aisle? Would it still count that he graduated if his diploma was received in the mail and thrown at the bottom of his closet under a forgotten pile of books, smelly t-shirts, and sports paraphernalia? Absolutely. I was totally at peace with that decision. This counselor struggled with that concept.

In hindsight, I have no doubt it was the right decision *not* to press this son to walk on graduation day with his high school peers. He didn't walk for high school. He didn't walk for college. But his sweet fiancé was able to convince him to walk when he graduated with his Master's in Apologetics. Yes, he got a degree in arguing! But at least it's in the defense of the Christian faith. Shocker, right? Our argumentative son found his niche in apologetics. Go figure. And he walked at commencement to celebrate his accomplishment. As his parents, we couldn't be prouder.

Let me be clear. Attaining peace doesn't happen naturally most of the time. We have to work at it. And the biggest advice I can give you to grab some heartfelt peace is to spend some time praising God.

To grab some heartfelt peace, spend some time praising God.

#SomeMiraclesNeedAMom | #AuthorSMcKeown

Exodus 15:2 (ESV) proclaims: "The Lord is my strength and my song, and he has become my salvation; this is my God, and I will praise him, my father's God, and I will exalt him." Thank him for being your defender when you become aware of his defense on your behalf and even when you haven't. *Sing* about his greatness. I especially like to put on praise music in my home. When no one is around, I crank that volume up and flood our home with praise music. It changes me when I praise him.

Mary had a different approach.

After Jesus was born, Luke observed: "But Mary treasured up all these things, pondering them in her heart."[45]

---

[45] Luke 2:19 (ESV)

Reflecting on what God has done is a good thing. It changes our attitude toward a more thankful process.

And, finally, keep in mind that the ultimate peace is having a right relationship with God.

"May the Lord give strength to his people! May the Lord bless his people with peace!"[46]

He gives strength to *his* people. He blesses *his* people with peace. Are you one of his people? If you're not, I challenge you to pick up a Bible and start reading to understand how to become one. Author Pricilla Shirer writes a piece of advice for such a time. She suggests we listen to God first thing in the morning " . . . while your heart is most open and refreshed and able to assimilate truth."[47]

It's worth the peace to try.

Are you experiencing God's peace today?

Why or why not?

If not, what steps will you take to discover His peace for you?

A simple prayer: *Lord, I am overcome with problems. I need your overwhelming peace today.*

---

[46] Psalm 29:11 (ESV)

[47] Priscilla Shirer, *Awaken* (Nashville: B & H Publishing Group, 2017) p. 4.

8

Mary Knew When to Get Out of the Way

Do you believe God can do what needs to be done?

When we have a child (or two or three) that we have to push, pull, and pray through multiple challenges, it's easy to become a helicopter parent. You know what I'm talking about. The parent that keeps hovering, watching for the first sign of *any* problem, even though all is well. They are always ready to swoop in and save the day. When this occurs on a regular basis, letting go gradually, or at all, becomes like the scene of an accident: it's as if you've engaged the brakes suddenly and sharply, leaving scars on the rhetorical pavement!

I put the brakes on my SUV rather quickly one morning. I had just dropped my daughter off at high school and, following the curved road in front of the school, heard a "clunk" on the passenger side of the vehicle. My eyes searched for the source of the noise and saw her forgotten clarinet, in its protective case, had tipped over while I was maneuvering the curve.

Several years earlier, I had made a stand *against* bringing forgotten items to school for her. I was trying to teach her responsibility, trying to get out of the way. But, on this day, it was obvious she had remembered to, at the very least, get it to the car. I had a moment of pity. I detoured back into the parking lot and, hurriedly, parked the car. I said a silent prayer of thanks that I had not driven her to school in the previous day's stay-at-home shabby outfit (although the current day's apparel was only a small improvement). I grabbed the instrument and jog-walked to the school's main office. Unfortunately, there was a line—a long one. I stood among the students, waiting for my turn to deal with the issue at hand. When it was my turn to talk to the very efficient tender of teen dilemmas for that day, I leaned forward and whispered my daughter's name, anxious for no one near to hear to whom the crazy looking lady belonged. The understanding soul at the desk seemed to comprehend immediately, nodding and answering in a lowered voice as well. I left grateful to be done with the drama.

But I was grateful too soon.

When I got back outside, I realized I had another dilemma: I had been focused on getting my daughter's clarinet inside the school when I parked the car. I had not paid attention to *where* I had parked. And, while I was standing in the long line in the office, at least a gazillion more cars had crowded into the lot. I had no clue where the SUV was.

I began walking up and down the rows of vehicles, again trying to avoid teens that might figure out that the weirdly dressed lady was connected with my daughter, when a police cruiser pulled up in front of me in the parking lot. The passenger window rolled down and the officer inquired, "May I help you, ma'am?"

I told him I had misplaced my car, and he questioned, "What kind of car is it?"

When I informed him of the make of the car I had driven that morning (I at *least* knew that), he countered, incredulously, "You just pulled in!"

Throwing out my arms, I reacted, "I know!"

Trying to help, he gave me a quick smirk: "I'll go this way and look for it."

I went in the opposite direction and breathed a huge sigh of relief when I was the one that found my car and not the oh-so-friendly-but-obviously-laughing-on-the-inside patrolman!

All this because I was trying to help with something I had once vowed I wasn't going to do anymore for my daughter.

We eventually need to learn to get out of the way so our children can move on to what they need to be doing.

Mary thought so. She recognized her Lord knew best. She stated her case at the wedding in Cana, possibly giving him a look that only a mother can pull off, and she walked away. She had faith that he could do it, and she trusted that he would do whatever he thought should be done.

Did she walk away knowing exactly what would happen? I doubt it. God's ways are mysterious. He could have made wine appear in infinite ways, or he could have chosen to stick with his initial timeline, delaying his first public miracle and not done as his mother had asked at all.

But Mary knew she'd done what *she* needed to do. Mary isn't mentioned again in the context of the wedding at Cana after she speaks the words, "Do whatever He tells you." That's it. She's outta there.

And, remember, she was asking on behalf of the family hosting the wedding, the people she loved who were facing possible embarrassment. She wasn't asking for anything for herself.

Neither was the mother of the sons of Zebedee. In Matthew 20:21b (ESV), the mother in the story came to Jesus for a favor. She said, "Say that these two sons of mine are to sit, one at your right hand and one at your left, in your kingdom."

"Jesus answered, 'You do not know what you are asking.'" (Matthew 20:22a [ESV])

This mom was seemingly jockeying for position for her two sons. She just wanted what was best for them, I'm sure. But sometimes we moms can be too bold. We ask for things that are far beyond our children's reach, or what God has intended for them.

Having "righteous" status as Christ-followers does not give us the authority to ask for a blank check. We can't ask for, or have, everything we want. Would we really choose that scenario, anyway? Don't we love a Father who disciplines us and teaches us to be responsible, just as we teach our own children? We would become spoiled, undisciplined creatures lacking any drive or goals if it were otherwise. Sometimes the heavy obligations directed our way are meant for us to either live with or deal with and get over them. I think Mary was prepared for all of those options. She had petitioned for the best outcome, but knew, deep down, not all requests are answered the way we would like.

When our son was first diagnosed with autism, I was disappointed we didn't have a quick answer. We had been taking him to different doctors in search of a solution, but simply found ourselves confronted with more problems as the diagnosis was confirmed. No one person could give us a probable, positive outcome. Some of the predictions professionals were making were institutional living or working on a simple assembly line; that was their "best case scenario." Don't get me wrong, assembly work must be done, but I had a different vision for my son. There was no quick resolution with this process. We were in it for the long haul. Being in it for the long haul was not the answer we wanted when we started asking questions.

When my husband asked me what he could do to help ease the load for the lengthy journey ahead, I asked him for two things: stay in town and take a yard job with the railroad instead of traveling out of town on freight trains, and take over the management of the checkbook.

He did both. (Have I mentioned God gave me a very good man?)

A year passed, and I was finally getting a little more sleep. I was also starting to feel like life was getting somewhat back to normal, albeit a new normal. I announced to my husband, who does not enjoy detail work, "I think it's time for me to take the checkbook back." It was a Saturday morning. I was sitting in the living room in my favorite flannel tent (a.k.a. nightgown), and he was sitting at the dining room table. After my declaration, he got out the checkbook and the calculator and started scratching figures—and his head. He'd punch a few more numbers and then scratch his head again.

I was watching all this quietly from across the room and was becoming a bit concerned.

Attempting to keep my voice calm, yet trying to be helpful, I piped up, "What was the number the last time you balanced the checkbook with the statement?"

"Statement?" He questioned.

With increasing concern, I pointed out, "They come in the mail with our bank's return address on them."

I watched as my husband's handsome face lit up with understanding. I was convinced we were, at last, on the same page. Until he said, "Oh, those! I filed them all, just like you do."

I then explained to him with rapid-fire words that I opened and processed them first! He responded: "That sounds like a lot of work."

He hadn't balanced the checkbook for the entire year. An. Entire. Year. We'd just been living (and spending) by faith. Which, by the way, is another miracle: we didn't overdraft our account the entire year!

I had a few words about how this was not the way we fly, and he came over to me, slid across the wood floor on his jean-clad knees the last few feet and, with complete sincerity, said, "I'm really sorry. What can I do?"

My response? "Bring me a calculator *with* a paper roll attached and get me some chocolate."

He did as I unmercifully demanded, and then I sat at the dining room table in my flannels for the next four hours, balancing the checkbook ledger for the year—*after* I had eaten the chocolate.

In retrospect, it sure would have been a whole lot easier to call the bank and inquire what our balance was (this was before online banking). My stubbornness was showing. And to be fair, I was managing the checkbook prior to this time because I was the one more gifted with attention to details. His heart just wasn't in it. The year before, he had taken on this role because I'd asked. He had tried to ease some stress for me, and he had. My stubbornness was not the gift he should have received for his sacrifice.

Walking away from the checkbook for a year was something I needed at that time. Was the work done the way I would have done it? Nope. Did our family survive the haphazardness of the year? Absolutely. Life doesn't always look like the Cleaver (*Leave It to Beaver*) home. Sometimes it looks more like the

Conner (*Roseanne*) household. And sometimes things just don't get done like *we* would have done them ourselves.

Could Mary have stayed close by and supervised the choreography of a miracle in progress? She could have. But I don't think she did. She did her part. She didn't stay close by to see *if* it was going to be done. She didn't stay close to see *how* it was going to be done. I believe she trusted what would be would be. She had the faith and confidence that Jesus had the power to act, and yet she understood the freedom he had to act *however* he deemed best.

God has the power and the freedom
to act *however* he deems best.

#SomeMiraclesNeedAMom | #AuthorSMcKeown

Bruce Wilkinson writes in *The Prayer of Jabez*:

Notice a radical aspect of Jabez's request for blessing; *He left it entirely up to God to decide what the blessings would be and where, when, and how Jabez would receive them.* This kind of radical trust in God's good intentions toward us has nothing in common with the popular gospel that you should ask God for a Cadillac, a six-figure income, or some other material sign that you have found a way to cash in your connection with Him. Instead, the Jabez blessing focuses like a laser on our wanting for ourselves nothing more and nothing less than what God wants for us.[48]

What does God want for us? He wants us to trust him. He wants us to want what *he* wants: a close relationship with him, relying on him for his vast power and decisions, not relying on our own limited understanding. He wants us to know we can go to him, fight for something different for our kids, but then get out of the way. When we do, we can relax, stop hovering, and trust God will do whatever is best.

Hudson Taylor writes: "Many Christians estimate difficulties in the light of their own resources, and thus attempt little and often fail in the little they attempt. All God's giants have been weak men who did great things for God because they reckoned on His power and presence being with them."[49]

There is a point in this process when we need to learn to let go of things we're not supposed to be hanging on to and allow God to do His will. He. Is. God. Trust him.

Sometimes the act of trusting isn't one simple step but many stepping stones.

---

[48] Bruce Wilkinson, *The Prayer of Jabez* (Sister, Oregon: Multnomah Publishers, 2000), p. 24.

[49] AZQuotes.com, Hudson Taylor Quotes.

At this writing, one of our adult sons doesn't communicate with the Conductor and me. There was a series of misunderstandings, which led to an email that caused the Conductor and me to first feel sick to our stomachs as we held each other and cried, and then pray for wisdom on how to respond.

Our answer was fivefold.

First, the Lord certainly knows what it feels like to be rejected by his own children: "He came to the people he created—to those who should have received him, but they did not recognize him."[50] There was comfort that he knew what we were going through, even though we were rejected on a much smaller scale than God ever had been or continues to be.

Second, God reminded me of one of my favorite verses that I had prayed throughout the years. Isaiah 49:25b says: " . . . for I will contend with those who contend with you, and I will save your children." I just never thought that one of those contending with me would be one of the children I had been praying for! But I also knew that God would know how to deal with my son much better than my husband and I ever could. God doesn't always deal with us gently. As much as I'd like to have positive results with my kids from a light touch, in reality, it doesn't always work that way.

Third, I was reminded of the story of the prodigal son:

> "There was a man who had two sons. And the younger of them said to his father, 'Father,

---

[50] John 1:11 The Passion Translation (TPT)

give me the share of property that is coming to me.' And he divided his property between them. Not many days later, the younger son gathered all he had and took a journey into a far country, and there he squandered his property in reckless living. And when he had spent everything, a severe famine arose in that country, and he began to be in need. So he went and hired himself out to one of the citizens of that country, who sent him into his fields to feed pigs. And he was longing to be fed with the pods that the pigs ate, and no one gave him anything. "But when he came to himself, he said, 'How many of my father's hired servants have more than enough bread, but I perish here with hunger! I will arise and go to my father, and I will say to him, 'Father, I have sinned against heaven and before you. I am no longer worthy to be called your son. Treat me as one of your hired servants.' And he arose and came to his father. But while he was still a long way off, his father saw him and felt compassion, and ran and embraced him and kissed him."[51]

On this third point, three facts stand out to me.

1. The father in this story allowed the son his sin; he didn't try to stop him. Getting out of the way can seem so hard! As we've raised

---

[51] Luke 15:11-20 (ESV)

our children, we've taught them right from wrong.

2. When our children are adults, *if* they want further instruction or advice, we, as their parents, should be available to give that to them. If, however, they are not interested in such input, our recourse is to be quiet and pray. It is not easy, but we need to get out of the way so we are not involved in the fight for a renewed life. It's between our child and God when they're adults. Eventually, in the story of the prodigal son, the son remembered his father's goodness. What a joy to have this occur!

3. The father was watching and waiting for his son's return. He saw his son while he was still far off. He watched, and hoped for his return, at all times.

The Conductor and I try to remember that we can't control how our son lives his adult life. We pray for the strength to stay quiet. And we watch for our son's return! We believe someday our son will remember that we love him.

Did we walk away from our son? No! But we *did* stop pursuing. There came a point when our actions were getting us nowhere. It was time to shut up and be quiet. Of course, we can pray while practicing silence.

Returning to the list, we come to answer four. The first couple of weeks after we received the previously referenced email from our son, we were what I would call "heartsick." We had scheduled a trip across country to visit this son, and his wife and children, but we were told we were not welcome. So . . . we scrambled to make alternate plans for our vacation, but our hearts weren't really in it. And, this all happened to be occurring around my birthday. The morning of my birthday, I woke up at our "Plan B" hotel, and I checked my emails and my Facebook page. I had a private message on my Facebook page from a gal from our church who had no clue what we were currently going through. I had never, up to that point, even sat down with her and had a cup of coffee. Here is what she wrote:

"Sandy, I didn't want to post this on Facebook for all to see, but this is so crazy! I woke up this morning at 4:30, and the Lord had you on my mind. I started to pray for you and sensed you needed encouragement." My encourager went on: "Oh how he loves you and sees you; the Lord smiles on you today." She continued, "And then . . . I went on my computer and saw it was your birthday today. Wow! What a God we serve!"

God knew the Conductor and I were in great pain. He knew when we were heartsick. I am so thankful I recognized his compassion and empathy, and I didn't brush off multiple friends' words of encouragement. I believe they were sent by him to ease our pain.

Finally, as the fifth part of our answer, I received a text from a good friend in our small group who was reading her Bible and felt compelled to share a verse with me. Proverbs 19:11 (ESV): "Good sense makes one slow to anger, and it is his glory to overlook an offense." We believe our son has been told lies about us from the ultimate enemy. As a result, our son has a skewed perception of our love for him. The Conductor and I have worked hard to overlook the offense of total rejection. It has *not* been easy.

Do you remember the scene in the movie *To Kill a Mockingbird* when the character Atticus, played by Gregory Peck, has been defeated as a lawyer? Atticus has attempted to clear a black man of crimes he did not commit at a time when segregation was very real. He has failed. His head is down as he walks out of the now empty courtroom. But up above in the balcony, the brothers and sisters, friends and neighbors of the accused all stand to give honor to the man who fought for their community, silently giving him his due. And during this scene, the preacher in the balcony admonishes Jem, Atticus' daughter, to stand, too. When she questions why, the preacher responds, "Because your daddy is walking past."

Jem did not value her father as the community of people did in that balcony. Our children do not see us as others do. Their perception is different. Perhaps they're more focused on our many failures, not seeing that we've tried our best. My husband and I have come to understand that.

We don't know how, where, or when the miracle of reuniting with our son will take place. We do know, though, that we need to stay out of the picture and wait for it to occur.

I never thought I'd be a parent that would have little contact with her child. I certainly never would have chosen it. In his book *Sacred Marriage,* author Gary Thomas writes, "Any situation that calls me to confront my selfishness has enormous spiritual value."[52] Even though marriage is the topic of the book, it certainly pertains to parenting as well. I mourn the gap between my son and me. Yes, I selfishly want that gap gone. But my husband and I have to set aside that selfishness and let it be. I believe pursuing our son and trying to explain ourselves would only make the situation worse.

Sometimes we just need to get out of the way—no matter how painful it feels.

> And Jesus answered them, "Have faith in God. Truly, I say to you, whoever says to this mountain, 'Be taken up and thrown into the sea,' and does not doubt in his heart, but believes that what he says will come to pass, it will be done for him. Therefore I tell you, whatever you ask in prayer, believe that you have received it, and it will be yours. And whenever you stand praying, forgive, if you have anything against anyone, so that your Father also who is in heaven may forgive you your trespasses." (Mark 11:22-25, ESV)

I've forgiven my son for the heartache he's caused, and I'm praying for the day I can visit with my grandchildren, who have, most certainly, no memory of me. There's even one (that we know of) I've never met. "...All things are possible for one who believes." (Mark 9:23b, ESV)

---

[52] Thomas, Gary. *Sacred Marriage* (Grand Rapids: Zondervan), p. 22.

If everything is possible, I pray for the strength to endure this separation.

Author Lailah Gifty Akita wrote, "May you always have extraordinary grace and faith to cope with the uncertainties of life."

Mary did.

Jesus had the power and freedom to act *however* he deemed best. Mary knew this. She walked away trusting for the best, knowing she had done everything she *should*.

Do what he tells you to do, then sleep well knowing you did everything you can.
The rest is up to God.
#SomeMiraclesNeedAMom | #AuthorSMcKeown

What have you been doing that you need to stop doing? Is there a situation in which you need to get out of the way?

Have you forgiven everyone you hold anything against?

A simple prayer: *"How would I discern the waywardness of my heart? Lord, forgive my hidden flaws whenever you find them."*[53]

---

[53] Psalm 19:12 (TPT)

"And when you stand praying, if you hold anything against anyone, forgive him, so that your Father in heaven may forgive you your sins."[54]

---

[54] Mark 11:25 (ESV)

9

Mary Had People

M ary directed the servants at the wedding to "... do whatever he tells you."[55] According to this biblical account, it appears the servants were standing by, ready to help at a moment's notice. Most likely, they'd been involved in preparations for the celebration of the marriage. Mary didn't have to go far to enlist help. Do you recognize who you have nearby to help you? Who has God put in your life to lend a hand with your circumstances? If you don't recognize these individuals or refuse to take them up on their offers to help, it's a whole lot harder to reach for that miracle.

Friends

One morning, my husband and I had a particularly difficult time dealing with one of our strong-willed sons. We eventually got him off to school, but couldn't agree on what our next steps should be. He was

---

[55] John 2:5b (ESV)

increasingly uncooperative, and resistant to ninety-nine percent of our parental directives. He was also just plain angry with us.

Should we force him into counseling? Should we continue just muddling through and hoping for the best? We stated our viewpoints to each other, then remained in a quiet stalemate, in separate rooms, for about forty-five minutes.

Then the kitchen phone rang.

The caller was a friend who checked with me on a regular basis to ask how things were going. She had been through much more difficult challenges with one of her own sons, and she had empathy, understanding, and encouragement for us. When she asked me how things were that day, I told her it was not a good day. She immediately asked me to meet her for lunch, but I told her I wasn't going to be able to go anywhere for lunch that day. I couldn't pretend and wear an "all is well" face out in public.

What she said next ultimately changed our family's story: "Then I'm coming over!"

And this sweet, kind, loving woman skipped her lunch break at work to come listen to our plight from that morning. I told her that my husband and I disagreed on how to proceed, and that he worried about making our son even madder by forcing him to go to counseling. This wise woman advised, "Don't make decisions based on whether it will make him *mad* or not. He's going to be mad no matter what you do. Make decisions based on whether it's *right* or not."

This was the push we needed.

It wasn't easy, but we eventually got that kid to go to counseling. Ironically, I think we learned more during those sessions than he did. We acquired a few more tools for our "parenting tool box," and, eventually, we achieved a little more peace in our home. We never would have accomplished any of that if our friend hadn't selflessly skipped her lunch that day to come over and give us a few words of wisdom—and a big dose of hope.

We *need* people that will listen and speak truth to us, who ultimately make a difference in our lives because they do.

Another Friend

Sometimes we need other people to help us see our children more clearly.

A friend came up to me at church one day, bubbly and full of joy. "I saw your handsome son walking the other day, and I stopped to offer him a ride," she said. "He is such a sweetheart! He's so polite and so nice to old ladies like me. You should be so proud!"

First, I was stunned that this strong-willed son—our Justice—who I did battle with on a daily basis, had been "nice and polite!" I certainly wasn't seeing that side of him at home.

Second, I was jealous. Why was he so nice to my friend when he was like a wet cat fighting to get out of a knotted gunny sack with my husband and me?

This woman's words gave me a glimpse of a son I didn't know, one who was kind, pleasant, and respectful. She gave me a glimmer of hope for my son and his future.

I repeat: sometimes we need other people to help us see our children more clearly.

These two women who offered words of encouragement and hope changed my family's story. They changed the lives of our children. They were part of the miraculous outcome for our family.

I could fill the rest of this book with stories of how people have helped us along our journey. One couple who own a pizza restaurant employed our kids, not because they had perfect skills for the job but because they were part of the church family. This couple was also good at loving us when we needed it most. They spent time with us, laughing, and sharing concerns about their kids while listening to our own.

Another couple, one of our associate pastors and his school social worker wife, was a perfect combination of wisdom, strength, and patience. These two were always ready to help, whether we asked them for advice or prayers concerning a new problem. After many years, we formed a great friendship with this couple. In fact, they were some of the first we called when my husband was diagnosed with melanoma and we needed someone to help process information with us. In the early days of our friendship, when this social worker friend was a casual acquaintance and we only saw each other in social settings, our two-year-old was diagnosed with autism. I remembered that this gal was on staff at the Area Education Agency and would be familiar with all the "lingo" the educators used. So, knowing I needed to use all the resources I had, I contacted her and asked her to a "walk and talk" with me. We would walk for exercise and then discuss what the "J-Team" (the moniker my husband gave the professionals that were assigned to us, most of their names started with 'J'—Joyce, Julie, Jane, Jan, John) would want for this son for the coming year. I had already done my research, carefully analyzing the options.

I wanted to make sure I could communicate clearly with his educators. I wanted to understand their terms, find out what to expect from them, be in agreement with this friend and the J-team when appropriate, and not be afraid to redirect them when necessary.

It worked.

My friend became such a good contact, I eventually invited her to the J-Team staffings (gatherings with professionals and parents to share information and set goals, sometimes writing, as a group, an IEP). During one such session, several of the J-Team members suggested that my friend should become a member of the autism team because she was so good at understanding and communicating the hurts and needs of our family. More importantly, she dreamed with us. When something was going right with our kids, she would point it out and encourage us with great enthusiasm. One day, the J-Team was at the house discussing options for our son. Several ladies were sitting in the living room, and while we were talking, the four-year-old we were discussing sat next to each person in turn and played his Game Boy.

He didn't interact with the ladies; his language was limited at the time. But my friend said: "Look! He's being social!" I wouldn't have noticed it if she hadn't pointed it out. On the flip side, she was one of the first to be outspoken enough to say to us, "What are you *thinking* here?" We all need friends who aren't too bashful to give us their honest opinions, don't we?

Now I'm thinking: we have had some amazing friends in our lives. They have helped us get through the valleys and have celebrated with us on our mountaintops.

I wasn't afraid to access the knowledge of people within my reach.

Who do you know? What can they do? It takes a church, community, and village to raise a child.

#SomeMiraclesNeedAMom | #AuthorSMcKeown

And One More

Back when we were a two-kid family, we added a third child with some trepidation. We had heard about the difficulties number three could pose. To reference a basketball/parenting strategy: You can't go "man-to-man" any longer; you have to go "zone." Changing defensive strategies was part of growing our parenting skills.

But despite our concerns, we were excited when we learned we would be bringing a third child into the family. When my delivery time arrived, my husband had taken our second son to his sister's house, just over an hour away, to stay during my hospitalization. After I had been back at home with the new baby for one day, we packed the diaper bag and drove to pick up this son. While we were at my sister-in-law's house, my husband got an unexpected call to go to work on a freight train much earlier than anticipated. We had to head back home immediately.

Once we got home, around eight that evening, the Conductor could do nothing to help me and the kids settle in. He needed to pack his grip (railroad term for duffle bag) and leave pronto.

In the meantime, I'd discovered that earlier in the day, before we had left town, my husband had stripped every bed in the house and had washed and dried all of the bedding. He hadn't redressed any of the beds. All of the linens were wadded together in a laundry basket. And now he didn't have time to do anything about it.

I was tired. The kids were tired. And most of us were crying. (I always hated the first time he left town after I'd had a baby). So, my wise husband paused as he was about to head out the door, looked at me with compassion, and said: "Call someone." He realized I needed reinforcements!

Of course! I'd have thought of it myself if I hadn't been so tired!

In tears, I called a friend who lived close by. She assured me she'd be right over, and she was. She walked in the door with a smile, her ever-present cup of coffee, and willing hands and feet. She asked what needed to be done and I babbled off the list through tears.

"Okay, I got it," she said. "You just sit there and take care of the baby."

So, I sat, fed the baby—and cried—while I listened to her accomplishing everything that—on any other day—I would have been able to do. She found the bedding and made all the beds. She got the two other kids ready for sleep, taking the time for a couple of bedtime stories and prayers as well. She comforted the son who missed his aunt, "I want Debbie!" If it had been up to me that night, they'd have gotten a "get to bed, I'll check on you in a little bit" bedtime routine. Poor kids.

There are times in life when stress is plentiful. It's during these times that we can count ourselves extremely blessed if helpful friends are plentiful, too.

Thankfully, in large families especially, there are times—particularly as the kids mature and get older—that you don't need to look outside of the immediate family unit for help.

Family

We were on our first major family vacation—near Durango, Colorado—after our youngest was born. (Those numbers sure change fast, don't they?) Our family was complete now: five kids, ranging from ages seventeen to one. We decided to park the car at the start of a trail and hike through some family-friendly routes.

It was a beautiful sunny day, and we were having a great time when our nine-year-old middle child had what we called an "episode." (At the time, we thought these episodes were migraines, based on what our family doctor had told us. Later, we found out that they were actually epileptic seizures). After these would occur, this son would be totally out of it and would sleep for several hours. That was never a problem when we were at home, but this was terrible timing: We were on a hiking trail and miles from the car.

At first, my husband carried our sleeping son on his back; then our older boys, the seventeen-year-old Leader, and the fifteen-year-old Wanderer, each took turns carrying their brother on their backs. About a mile from the car, all three were totally exhausted. They'd each taken several turns, and our recovering son was still half asleep. My husband's weariness was evident on his face. To this point, I had been carrying our youngest, the baby, in a pack on my back, but I decided to try taking a turn carrying our still unconscious son on my back. I handed the baby to our youngest son and took my turn with our groggy child. It was hard. Each step on the trail became more difficult with the burden I was now carrying. I felt like we were never going to reach our destination, and I didn't even carry him very far. My husband took another turn after he'd gotten some rest.

We finally made it to the car, and we did it as a team.

That's what family is all about.

We worked together, traveling through the fun part of life and, when the path to fun quickly changed to a path of trial, we carried the burden as a team. When the trail turns to trial, it's good to have a family.

We can't do life successfully alone.

#SomeMiraclesNeedAMom | #AuthorSMcKeown

Faith

I can't count how many prayers went unanswered as we raised our five.

"Help him, Lord, to be a little easier to deal with today."

"Can this day be a little easier than yesterday, Lord?"

"Dear Lord, I just need some peace!"

In my desperation, these were prayers for an easier day, but I believe God was allowing things to occur that would ultimately take our family to a different destination: a God-honoring life. If any one of those prayers had been answered, I don't believe I would have taken such a strong stand with my husband for counseling that morning with our strong-willed Justice when it was so necessary. Those prayers for ease of the day were not answered, I believe, because God has something else for us. It was part of the process, getting us to the point where he wanted us.

In the Book of John the disciples ask Jesus, " . . . Rabbi, who sinned, this man or his parents, that he was born blind?" Jesus answered, "It was not that this man sinned, or his parents, but that the works of God might be displayed in him."[56]

I do not believe my children were born with learning challenges because of sin. What I *do* believe is that the work of God will be displayed in their lives because of what he did in and through them. We didn't go through those dark valleys for nothing. He had a purpose: so that he would be glorified. Many may not understand this concept of allowing difficulty so that God can be honored.

The Conductor certainly understands the "difficulty" part. My husband has the patience of a saint, especially with a wild-eyed, stressed, overtired wife. But he often used his playful tendencies to lighten a dark mood. One day his humor was especially prevalent. He was in a mood to tease me relentlessly! By the time we got into bed that night, I warned him I had a strong urge to whack him with the book I was reading. He calmly asked, "What's the name of the book?" I told him, "*The Jesus-Hearted Woman*." We both laughed. Obviously, if I was threatening my husband with whacking him, my heart needed some more molding!

---

[56] John 9:2b-3 (ESV)

125

There were so, so many times when I realized God was right: *two are better than one.*[57] My spouse labored alongside me. He steadied me. He brightened the dark days. And he reminded me often: *it's going to be okay.*

Would the miracle at the wedding have occurred without other people helping? I don't believe it would have. *Someone* needed to fill the jars to the brim with water. *Someone* needed to draw some water out and take it to the master of the banquet to taste. And *someone* needed to recognize that other people can help.

Do you have people in your life who can help you toward your miracle? Or are you trying to pursue a miracle alone?

A simple prayer: *Lord, I recognize these problems I'm facing are more than what I can possibly face alone. Please help me recognize those who can help me face these trials, those who will have answers that I need. And, Lord, please create in me a heart ready to hear.*

---

[57] Ecclesiastes 4:9 (ESV)

10

All In

Heading home one hot summer day, I decided to take the backroads due to excessive traffic on the main highways. I was enjoying the much quieter roads, feeling pleased with myself for remembering to avoid all the commotion on the construction-clogged interstate, when I navigated a curve and saw a lone doe standing right in the middle of the road. Not moving. Still as could be. I had plenty of time to slow down and stop; it was a fluke she had positioned herself to allow for a strategic stop of my car. Or was it?

Animals didn't always fear humans. Their fear of us came after the flood: "The fear of you and the dread of you shall be upon every beast of the earth . . ."[58] I'm sure God had his reasons; preservation of animal life probably being one of them. I had no doubt this creature feared me, but what was she up to?

I slowed to a gentle stop about seven feet from her, and we locked eyes. Her big, beautiful doe eyes

---

[58] Genesis 9:2a (ESV)

did not move even a little. "Okay, what's the plan here?" I voiced aloud, even though I knew she couldn't hear or understand me. Then I saw movement out of the corner of my eye in the ditch to the left. A gangly newborn that had not yet learned to walk very gracefully climbed out of the ditch with considerable effort and noisily scrambled across the road, lanky legs working hard. The fawn stumbled a little along the way, and then disappeared into the reeds and shrubbery on the other side of the road. Once the newborn was safe, the doe broke eye contact with me and quickly followed her young. They were both out of sight in seconds.

This beautiful momma had flagged traffic for her baby.

It was a powerful example to me of momma fierceness, forgetting what fear you have in the moment because it's time to fight for your baby—at any cost.

That momma was what I would call "all in" for her baby. She would do anything for her offspring. She would give her very own life if she had to. Being the best mom she could be, at least for that moment, was an *all-in* venture.

Yep. I knew *exactly* what that momma deer was doing. I understood her courage, her tenacity, and her instinct to do whatever it took to help her baby survive this thing called life. She was fighting for her baby's future.

The beasts of the earth fear man. This doe feared me and, I'm sure, the large vehicle I was driving, but she stood her ground. She had somehow, tragically, learned that cars kill. And she was doing something fearsome to protect her baby.

She was willing to face something that could hurt her. With heart racing, lungs-aren't-getting-enough-air kind of fear. Wishing you didn't have to do it, but there is no other choice kind of fear. She knew it was necessary to protect her baby.

Author Mark Batterson wrote a book titled *All In*. The synopsis on the back of this book starts: "The gospel costs nothing, but it demands everything. It's all or nothing."[59]

He's got an excellent point. It reminds me of parenting. If we are blessed with children, then we have a responsibility to raise these children the best we know how. Kids demand everything from us. It's all or nothing. We don't have the luxury of "phoning in" our parenting duties if we want our kids to have a quality life.

Mary, the mother of Jesus, was an all-in kind of mother.

After Mary had exited the scene at the wedding in Cana, servants were in play: "Now there were six stone water jars there for the Jewish rites of purification, each holding twenty or thirty gallons. Jesus said to the servants, 'Fill the jars with water.' And they *filled them up to the brim*."[60]

Notice these jar were filled to the brim. Not part way. Not till they *felt* it was enough. Filled. To the brim!

---

[59] Mark Batterson, *All In* (Grand Rapids: Zondervan, 2013).
[60] John 2:6-7 (ESV)

If we want a healthy outcome, we need a healthy amount of input. We need to be all in.

And, hey, I get it. Life can be so difficult sometimes. The hosts at the wedding in Cana could have embarrassingly announced that they were closing down the festivities earlier than planned due to "unforeseen circumstances." But Mary devised a plan. These were people she loved and cared about. She wasn't giving up.

We can often be tempted to quit. There have been times...

Our oldest son and his wife lived in Colorado when they were newlyweds. They couldn't come to us for Thanksgiving one year, so we drove the nine hours to them. They had just moved into their first home, which created a bit of chaos when combining extended family, a holiday, and shopping for dresses for another son's upcoming wedding. While there for the five-day duration, our caravan broke down. After discovering the extent of the issue, it was decided the vehicle was not worth fixing. We had it towed away and rented a car to drive back home. A snow and ice storm was also brewing as we were leaving, and our youngest child had caught the flu. The combination of the stressors was palpable.

My husband was driving. Our Justice, who didn't like being cramped, was in the front passenger seat of the much smaller economy car than what we had driven *to* Colorado. Determined was sitting to my left in the back. I was sitting in the middle, and our daughter was sprawled on my lap, an empty ice cream bucket strategically poised for what might come next.

The trip was taking much longer than usual due to ice on the roads. Several cars were in the ditches on both sides of the highway. Traffic was cautiously crawling.

My husband worked nights at the time and was supposed to go to work at eleven that night. He was feeling the pressure to keep going, but we were all tired. He was just about ready to throw in the towel and call it quits when I got the idea to call my brother. In all actuality, I'm pretty sure it was God who gave me the idea. After all, I'd been praying since we'd left our grown son's driveway!

I called my brother and explained where we were and that road conditions had deteriorated. We wanted to know what the weather maps were saying. (This was before all our phones got so smart). He said he'd look online and give me a call back.

He called within just a few minutes. "You're in the worst of it, but you're almost out of it. You've got about another ten miles or so, and you'll be able to pick up speed and head home safely."

You're almost out of it.

It was exactly what we needed to hear.

We could keep going knowing that we were near the end of our chaotic, most difficult, not-so-fun holiday trip ever.

We arrived home safely. My husband quickly changed for work and headed out, and I dealt with exhausted (and sick) kids. It was the best outcome for the moment. It wasn't pretty, but we did what needed to be done.

We can't always hear directly from a brother, a parent, or a friend that "we're almost out of it" and to keep going. But we can turn to a Father who is always there and always hears when we're in our life's plights.

Don't quit!

Keep moving!

When we're all in, giving up is not an option.

While my husband and I were raising our kids, it was a full-on effort by both of us. Our pastor of fourteen years once asked my husband if he had any hobbies; my husband responded: "My kids *are* my hobbies."

With five kids, there wasn't a lot of time for anything else while they were growing up. The Conductor was an *all-in* dad. I am so grateful for this character trait in him!

When it comes to our kids, giving up is not an option.

#SomeMiraclesNeedAMom | #AuthorSMcKeown

What prompted us to go all in?

After the birth of our first child, I bought a ton of parenting books. I read them all, hoping to gain wisdom on how to do this thing right. I wasn't quite sure I was up for the challenge. To be honest, I felt pretty inadequate. I needed to learn more. As we added each additional child, we discovered that all the books didn't have all the answers. We were going to be "winging it with Jesus" a whole lot.

My husband attended a private school throughout his elementary years, and he wanted the same for our kids. It's easy to send one to part-time kindergarten and pay for it, but when there are four attending all day, every day, the financial burden of having them all in private school is more difficult. It wasn't easy. Most people have a mortgage payment as their biggest bill. Ours was the kids' tuition bill. Following behind came the grocery bill (four boys) and *then* came our mortgage. We chose to live in a much smaller house so we could afford tuition for our kids. (We stacked 'em!)

Later on, when they were going off to college one by one, we promised we would pay for half of their college tuition *if* they maintained a B average. (I know! I know! It's contrary to financial planners' rules to pay for college before retirement is saved for, but the railroad has a pension plan that we felt would make a difference for us so we could make a difference for our kids). Most of our kids made us pay up. (Darn kids!) We drove cars until they would no longer run. We didn't go on expensive trips. When we did travel, we stayed with family and friends. We were *all in* on parenting. At this writing, we just celebrated making our last payment to the last college. We've been making those payments to various colleges for eighteen years due to the age spread of our kids.

That's a long time to be parenting. (Our youngest moved out of our house and into her first apartment three days after her oldest brother turned thirty-nine. That's thirty-nine years with kids under our roof!)

But finances and time aren't the only *all in* qualities. When our "normal" family life was disrupted by several behavior diagnoses that, we were told, would affect our family—and three of our four sons—for the rest of their lives, there were decisions to make. Would we take the professionals' word for it?

Or would we find the strength to do something different to affect the outcome for these sons?

My desire to pursue something different for our sons was strong. There was a motivation to do something that would make a difference in their lives. Again, reading books, discovering what to do so I could become a better parent, were motivators for me to go all in.

And going all in for one son taught us how to go all in for the next son as well. When a problem arose down the road for one of our other kids, we came to a much quicker solution each successive time that involved going *all in*. Each diagnosis ended up helping us become more involved in the parenting process.

But I truly believe that *all in* wouldn't have made a bit of difference if I hadn't been *all in* for my Lord.

In Mark Batterson's book, he writes: "You don't get to know God by looking at him from a distance."[61] And if we don't know him, and can't hear him, what do we do so we can get those answers? We move closer to him.

Have you ever seen a far away train? It looks small and you can't hear any sound. But as it moves closer, you realize how very large and powerful it actually is and, as it continues to move closer, you can hear the roar of its massive engines and feel the unmistakable vibration of the ground as its linked railcars speed by. Your perspective of that train changes as it moves closer.

Our perspective of God changes when we get closer to him, too. And, if we're close enough, we *want* to be all in.

Batterson goes on: "We all want to spend *eternity* with God. We just don't want to spend *time* with Him. We stand and stare from a distance, satisfied with superficiality. We Facebook more than we seek His face. We text more than we study The Text. And our eyes aren't fixed on Jesus."[62]

Dear God, I've been guilty of that entire paragraph. I need to move closer.

Do you?

How did Mary discover there was no more wine at the wedding? Scholars tell us she was most likely helping to serve at the wedding, probably because

---

[61] Mark Batterson, *All In*, (Grand Rapids: Zondervan, 2013), p. 77.

[62] Mark Batterson, *All In* (Grand Rapids: Zondervan, 2013), p. 77.

the hosts were relatives. In all likelihood, she saw the empty jars for herself. But then she had a decision to make: would she do anything about it?

She needed to go *all in* for the people she loved.

When people say I'm an exceptional parent, I guarantee them I'm not. My kids would not be the successes they are today if I had not pursued my Lord and my God on their behalf. *He* showed me how to get off the easy route. *He* showed me how to advocate for my kids. It was an all-in venture to the highest degree.

And it changed the outcome for my kids.

If you pursue God on behalf of your kids, I guarantee it will change their lives. Are you ready to go all in on your kids' behalf?

What steps do you need to take to be more *all in*?

A simple prayer: *Dear Lord, fill our emptiness to the brim! Give me the strength and wisdom to do everything I need to do for my kids.*

11

God Uses Old, Empty Vessels

"Jesus said to the servants, 'Fill the jars with water.'"[63]

The stone jars were old vessels, typically used for washing. And they were empty. They had been used for washing because "Jews became ceremonially defiled during the normal circumstances of daily life, and were cleansed by pouring water over the hands. For a lengthy feast with many guests a large amount of water was required for this purpose."[64]

Defiled—tainted, tarnished—during the normal circumstances of daily life. That certainly sounds familiar, doesn't it?

Repeated repentance—a soul cleansing, if you will—as we live our lives is certainly part of the solution.

---

[63] John 2:7 (ESV)
[64] John 2:6 Study Notes, *The NIV Study Bible* (Zondervan, Grand Rapids, MI, 1995).

137

But we also need to make room for the good things God has for us. Have you left behind the past, the bitterness, the pain that you have accumulated just by walking on this earth? Everyone has *stuff*. No one is alone on that front. Let's be honest: life can be hard sometimes. We need to make deliberate, healthy choices to get beyond that hard stuff and grow. Once we do, I believe we will become a person who can do more on this earth than we ever dared dream. By letting go, we make room to grow. We also make room for miracles.

In the beginning of this book, I gave an example of a clenched-fisted prayer. Are you ready to pray with an open palm?

Dear Lord,
Forgive me for trying to do things my way.
I finally understand my way won't work.
Help me to understand
Your wisdom and your ways.
All that I am, all that I have, I give to you.
I'm yours.

Simple, right?

I have struggled with depression off and way-too-much on for most of my mothering years.

When the depression is more "on" than "off," it's an emotional, mental, spiritual, and physical heaviness that permeates my existence and is present immediately when waking up in the morning. It's a blanket of gloomy darkness that follows wherever I go. It's a fight to get out from under it. And, at times, the combined weight of the heaviness of the depression and the turmoil my family was in meant I wasn't fighting very effectively.

In the midst of the bedlam of strong-willed children, sleepless nights, a traveling husband, and the myriad of problems that having children with multiple issues present, I was fighting crisis fatigue and a personal battle with depression that just wouldn't leave me alone.

In the Book of Mark there is an account of a parent who was struggling due to *his* son's problems:

And Jesus asked his father, "How long has this been happening to him?"

And he said, "From childhood. And it has often cast him into fire and into water, to destroy him. But if you can do anything, have compassion on us and help us."

And Jesus said to him, "'If you can'! All things are possible for one who believes."

Immediately the father of the child cried out and said, "I believe; help my unbelief!"[65]

Author Craig Groeschel writes: " . . . this dad was at the end of his rope. After doing everything he could think to do, it's possible that he'd finally resigned himself to despair and loss."[66]

I never got to the point of despair and loss *for my kids*—God always gave me a special strength to keep

---

[65] Mark 9:21-24 (ESV)
[66] Craig Groeschel, *Hope in the Dark* (Grand Rapids: Zondervan, 2018), p. 18.

fighting for them—but I did get to a point of despair and loss for *myself*.

Have you ever given up on a diet? Yeah . . . me, too. In that moment, we are frustrated with the lack of progress and convinced that we will never get out from under the weight of it, literally, so we give up trying.

There were many mornings that I woke with the all-too-familiar depressive heaviness. The combined weight of the depression and the almost ever-present cacophony of chaos in our family tempted me to stay in bed with the covers pulled over my head.

But how would that have helped?

Most married couples eventually use "shorthand" phrases to communicate things quickly. For the Conductor and I, a mention of "the ostrich method" was a shorthand way of saying: "Pick up your head and face what we need to face!"

I felt alone, unworthy to do what was needed of me, and so unsure of how I was going to make it through—not just the years ahead—but that *one day*. *Every day* during that season. At times, if felt like the day was taunting me with its bright sun and the happy birds chirping merrily.

Oswald Chambers writes: "My vision of God is dependent upon the condition of my character. My character determines whether or not truth can even be revealed to me."[67]

In my darkness, little truth was getting through.

But my Lord had a plan . . .

---

[67] Oswald Chambers, *My Utmost For His Highest* (Grand Rapids: Discovery House Publishers, 1992, Updated Version), July 13.

The SON Revealed

I had been asked by a group of educational professionals to join a team that was comprised of both professionals that worked with special needs kids and parents that were raising special needs kids. We would get together and discuss what was working and what wasn't in the education system. As part of this team, I was offered a chance to attend a statewide seminar with a minimum of personal financial cost.

Despite experiencing a pretty deep depression, I had arranged to have my in-laws come babysit the four boys so I could drive across the state to attend my first-ever conference for parents of special needs children. I had no idea what to expect and later discovered I wasn't alone in my struggles. Of course, subconsciously, we all know we aren't alone, but hearing about the struggles of others somehow encourages us. I learned a lot at the conference, but the presenters also challenged us to deal with our emotions. I was tired. Still depressed. And it was time to go home.

I prayed: Oh, Lord, give me strength to do what needs to be done back home!

I packed my suitcase, walked out to the parking lot, and discovered the fog was so thick it was eerie.

I had driven a rental due to our car being in the shop, and I was unfamiliar with the buttons and knobs on the rental's dash and the radio was not pre-set to my favorite stations. The fog was thick. I literally could only see headlights coming at me. I concentrated on keeping to the *right* of each successive pair of lights shining dimly amid the thick ground cover as I drove carefully home.

I was pushing buttons on the car, trying to find a station that was playing something that would keep me company as I traveled. I couldn't see another human being, so it felt like I was the only person on the planet; I felt so alone. A voice on the radio would be most welcome.

I was coming across predominantly static. None of my familiar stations seemed to be getting through. Google reports: "Water (in this case in the form of fog) is an electrical conductor, and absorbs radio waves. The effect will be to reduce signal strength, which can cause a digital signal to break up . . ."[68] I assumed that was the cause for the many channels of static.

But God has mysterious ways.

I finally came across a station that was playing a familiar song. The chorus was just ending when I pulled my hand away from the knob and returned it to the steering wheel. Then the radio announcer came on the air. In his smooth, baritone voice, he said: "Today's verse is Psalm 40, verse 2: 'He lifted me out of the slimy pit, out of the mud and mire; he set my feet on a rock and gave me a firm place to stand.'"[69] And then the radio returned to static.

It felt like God had sent that message directly to me.

---

[68] Google.com; *Can weather affect radio waves?* October 4, 2018.

[69] Psalm 40:2 *Holy Bible*, New International Version (New York: International Bible Society, 1978).

I began to sob and praise him simultaneously as I maneuvered the car around winding roads toward home.

It was still quite foggy outside, but I was having a church experience with my Lord inside the car! Praising God, singing, sobbing my thankfulness for his promise of hope that was *just* what I needed to hear.

But then . . . something else happened. The fog suddenly lifted, and the sun was shining—but on the wrong side of my face! I was headed in the wrong direction! In the midst of my journey in the fog, I had missed a needed turn. I wouldn't be getting to my desired destination if I continued going this way.

And then I realized: I had felt so alone in that fog, but when the fog lifted the sun was still there. Just as when that depression lifts, the SON is still shining, for those that are looking. He's there whether we see him or not.

He'd been waiting for me.

I got the car turned around and arrived home safely that day. The fog had cleared, and my part of the world looked familiar again. But *I* was different. The Lord had met me in my personal, dark place and given me hope. It was the beginning of the ease of the depression. And I came home with new energy for the task at hand: raising my kids.

I wish I could tell you my life was all "smooth roads ahead" after this experience. It wasn't always. Keeping my focus on God in the midst of my problems was something I needed to learn.

Unfortunately, I've had to keep relearning that.

I needed to grow my strength in God to accomplish the task of raising my kids and making wise decisions for them.

Growing Through Mistakes

One day, when Justice was about two months old, he and I had both tried to have it "our way" repeatedly in the nursing process. Neither of us were successful. We fought each other through the entire undertaking. We just didn't make a good nursing team. The Conductor was due home soon from out of town, so I planted myself in the living room in a rocking chair, holding my just-fed, freshly diapered infant son, determinedly waiting for my husband's imminent return. When he arrived, I held Justice up to him as soon as he crossed the threshold and firmly said: "Here, take him. I don't want to see him until it's time to feed him again."

My husband's response was to ignore the wild-looking, exhausted woman in the rocking chair and focus with a smile solely at our son. With a singsong voice, he ignored my words and gently picked up our baby, cradling him tenderly in the crook of his arm. "Who could possibly be upset with you?"

Humph!

This incident, I believe, began the process of the Conductor bonding with Justice in a totally different way than with any of our other five children. Justice ended up favoring the Conductor over me while still a baby. This was our first, and only, child to do this. The other three boys and our one and only Princess favored me when they were little and then gradually their dad became their favorite. I have my own suspicions about the reasons why. Perhaps because he was gone so much for work, it contributed to him saying "yes" much more often than I did. But it is not a bad thing for them to favor the man I chose to be married to for life. Their dad is a very good man, someone I am not upset at all that they gravitate to and emulate.

Unfortunately, the Conductor was so pleased to have a child that preferred him early on, he declined to discipline him later when he needed it.

Years later, when we were in counseling with this son, now a strong-willed teenager, the counselor encouraged the Conductor to engage with the discipline process. My husband literally responded by looking at his watch and saying, "We've got eighteen months, four days, and twenty-seven minutes of him left in the house. I'm good with things as they are."

Whoa!

I shot the counselor that resigned look of, "See what I'm dealing with here?!"

But when I calmed down, I realized *I* needed to be the one to get out of the way in this process. I had been handling all of the discipline, partly because he had traveled so much. Our counselor pointed out that it was time to make some changes.

Had we finally both reached the point where we were miserable enough to stop getting things "our way" and do what was best for our family? For our kids?

Many years earlier my husband had recounted a story of his grandfather, who was also a railroad man. Back in his day, there were no workers' unions. The crews could be assigned to a train and take it from one coast to the next. There were no limits to how long they could be on duty. So, they could often be gone for weeks at a time.

Back home, my husband's grandmother was raising five boys in a two-bedroom house while her man was working, eating, and sleeping on a caboose on the rails. She was a traditional woman of the time who believed her husband should be the head of the house—and, consequently, the sole disciplinarian. So, when her husband got back home after being gone so long, she would rattle off the list of infractions each boy had committed in their father's absence. And those infractions each deserved a "walloping."

But when her husband would arrive home after his long journey, all the boys knew what was coming and would "dive" for cover, afraid of their impending punishments.

One day my husband's grandfather emphatically declared he'd had enough of that arrangement. He told his wife, "The boys don't even want to see me when I get home. I'm done disciplining them for things they do when I'm not here. From now on, *you* do it."

My father-in-law remarked that was the worst thing to happen to him and his brothers. He remembers how his dad, when doling out the punishment, was pretty easy on them. His heart just wasn't in it. But when his mother had gotten the "go-

146

ahead" to administer the spankings, her heart was in it, and each instance was just a bit more memorable!

The Conductor shared this story with me to establish a family precedent had been set. He would travel, and I would discipline *while he was gone*. But we eventually got away from that arrangement. When he got back home, I would need to inform him, or even leave post-it notes, of who was grounded from which activity. For example, on the TV: "(The Leader) is grounded from this until . . . " and then the date would be included on it. But, in the chaos of life, it became a burdensome communication that we unknowingly abandoned. As a result, I became almost the sole disciplinarian. The Conductor rarely took part. The counselor we were seeing pointed it out to us and stated: "Having Mom wear the pants works for compliant children, but it makes no sense to strong-willed children."

I needed to step back and get out of the way—again!

A crisis reveals much about us. This crisis revealed I still had a lot of dross—unwanted junk—in my life that I needed to get rid of.

David writes in Psalms: "The sacrifices of God are a broken spirit; a broken and contrite heart, O God, you will not despise."[70] It is notable this Psalm was written *after* David had committed sin—adultery this time. He certainly knew what a broken spirit and contrite heart felt like.

---

[70] Psalm 51:17 (ESV)

How do we attain the contrite heart he's talking about?

My pastor once shared an example during his sermon regarding sin. He said sinning is like throwing a big handful of sand up in the air. What happens when we do that? The sand comes right back down on top of us, but scattered. Those in our inner circle of people, those closest to us, experience the consequences of that sand/sin coming down on them the most. Those in our outer circles get less sand/sin on top of them, but they still feel the effects of it.

How long can we sin if we think no one else is affected? I think we can sin an ugly long time. It's pretty hard to stop throwing sand if there are no perceived consequences. But when we realize those around us will be affected by our sin, it should change everything. When we're ready to stop the sin, whatever it may be, a repentance takes place that empties us of all that *we* want to do. We've had enough. We don't want to cause pain anymore.

Once we've been broken and emptied, we're ready to be used by God.

I stepped back and allowed my husband to manage our strong-willed son those last eighteen months (and four days!) in our home. Was it a smooth transition? No. Did my husband pick up the task and run with it without problems? Absolutely not. But we muddled through it and reached our goal: Justice graduated and moved out of our house to learn more about life beyond what we could teach him at that time.

When he moved out, we were still broken and empty. We were shocked by the quietness in our home after his departure. But peaceful serenity didn't come until we dealt with our own inadequacies as parents and forgave each other for the reactions that caused more problems than eased them.

One of my reactions that we could have done without? I didn't properly take care of myself through the season of raising five kids.

Learning More

I. Am. A. Stress. Eater. There—I said it. I comfort myself when I am under stress by eating food. It's the easy See-Food diet. I eat whatever food I see. When the kids were all in their toughest phases, it would often take me two hours to get them all to bed, settled down, and asleep while my husband was out of town. I would slip out of the last child's bed I had rotated to, tip-toe to the stairway, and be rifling through the food options in my mind by the time I reached the landing, trying to decide if I was going to start with something crunchy and salty or something smooth and sweet for my evening treat. It didn't really matter, of course. I was going to just *start* with one texture and *move on* to the other texture in the same sitting!

After laundry day, when I'd pull clean clothes out of the closet to wear, and they didn't fit as they had before, I was sure it was the dryer's fault. I was quite positive it was shrinking all my clothes!

But I was lying to myself. I could blame the dryer all I wanted. But I was the one making the choice to comfort myself in the wrong manner. I should have been turning to my Lord, the great Comforter, to help me get through a season in my life that had me exhausted, desperate, and sleep deprived until I was physically nauseous. Oh sure, I went to church on Sunday. I prayed on the go and listened to some uplifting music once in a while, but I wasn't getting to the bottom of my hurts. I needed to be desperate *for* my Lord, not desperate just *because* of my woes.

During this time, I was visiting at a friend's house with a few girlfriends on a beautiful summer evening. This friend was a no-nonsense kind of gal that was a natural Violet Crawley—long before *Downton Abbey* ever came across the airwaves. We were sipping iced teas and enjoying an abundance of laughs and an overall great time until, at one point, I excused myself to use the bathroom. While in there, I noticed a scale. Back home, the kids had broken my scale a long time ago. I couldn't remember the last time I had stepped on one of those things. (Probably at my post-natal checkup after the youngest child was born!) I eyed it. I contemplated stepping on it. And I decided I was curious enough to risk it. After emptying my bladder, which all women know to do before stepping on a scale, I bravely stepped on. And screamed!

My "Violet" nearby in the kitchen called out, "What's wrong?"

"I stepped on the scale!" I yelped.

"Well, get off it!" she blatantly instructed, in her best "Violet" tone.

But the damage was done. I now knew how much I weighed. The scale had revealed to me what I had refused to believe after seeing my reflection in too many mirrors. I was astounded how much weight I had gained and recognized the reason without too much pondering: I was comforting myself in ways that just weren't healthy.

On the drive home that evening—in which I was markedly subdued after stepping on the scale—I sang a familiar song from liturgy, taken from Psalm 51:10-12, "Create in me a clean heart, O God; and renew a right spirit within me. Cast me not away from thy presence; and take not thy holy spirit from me. Restore onto me the joy of thy salvation, and uphold me with thy free spirit."[71]

I was broken. But now I needed to be empty of the things that were hindering me.

As the jars were empty at the wedding in Cana and the tomb was empty at Jesus' burial site, I now needed to make room for what God had in mind for whatever was next in my life. And, I learned, somewhat frustratingly, that this is a recurring thing. It's not something I process once and then move on with my life and all is well. I must repent often and move forward with confidence that the dregs of my heart have been cleaned out and I can be used for the purposes of God. This is the miraculous power of repentance and hope offered to all!

---

[71] Psalm 51:10-12 King James Version (KJV) of the Bible

Make room for what God has in mind
for what is next.

#SomeMiraclesNeedAMom | #AuthorSMcKeown

Jesus can transform what is inside old containers; the ones previously filled with dirty sin become clean and filled with the renewing works of God!

He washes away the residue of uncleanness and makes something new. And it's often the best ever! "When the master of the banquet tasted the water now become wine, and did not know where it came from (though the servants who had drawn the water knew), the master of the feast called the bridegroom and said to him, 'Everyone serves the good wine first, and when people have drunk freely, then the poor wine. But you have kept the good wine until now.'"[72]

Imagine what we can do, the accomplishments we can reach, when we get rid of the junk and fill ourselves with the miraculously new of God.

Are you ready to get rid of the junk in your life? Do you recognize what the dregs are from?

---

[72] John 2:9-10 (ESV)

A simple prayer: "*Create in me a clean heart, O God, and renew a right spirit within me. Cast me not away from thy presence; and take not thy holy spirit from me. Restore unto me the joy of thy salvation; and uphold me with thy free spirit.*"[73]

---

[73] Psalm 51:10-12 (KJV)

12

Mary's Faith Quenched the Thirsty

I would have loved to sit across from Jesus' mother, Mary, at her wooden kitchen table. Perhaps it was lovingly handmade by her husband, Joseph, a carpenter by trade. Would the worn spots on her table reflect the activities performed there? Perhaps worn spots were evident in the area where she made bread. Perhaps there was a worn spot where she sat and prayed fervently for wisdom as she was learning and being stretched as a mother. What was this amazing woman like? After finding out she was expecting her first child, she hurried off to visit with her cousin Elizabeth. How many women hurried off to visit with *her* after receiving life-altering news? Can you imagine sitting across the table and learning from this amazing woman?

It's a privilege to sit with a person who has some wisdom of God. There is an inherit hope that maybe we, too, will receive some of the favor they have received. Maybe, just maybe, they'll tell of their journey as a new believer into one who walks in strong faith.

I know Mary had a close relationship with her son. She couldn't have successfully pursued that miracle in Cana if she hadn't. Surprised? I'll explain.

Have you ever read a rant on social media? Someone is not happy—they didn't get their way—and they go on a rant, blaming God for their circumstances?

Yeah. I have, too.

They lay out how some evil has occurred; I don't disagree with that part of their rant. I have no doubt what happened is an evil thing. But when they blame God, I question their reasoning. Do they recognize and honor God during the days when all is going well? Do they have a relationship with him when the pressure is off and the sun is shining brightly? Is God allowed to be recognized as the one true God in their home? Do they acknowledge him as Lord of their life? When you exclude Someone from your life, pursuing life in your own way without that Someone, yet blame that same Someone for not succeeding in your pursuits, does it make sense?

Yeah, I don't think so, either.

Mary had a righteousness that came from God through faith in Jesus. Mary's righteousness, her relationship with her Lord and the faith He gave her that bestowed righteousness on her, made a difference in other people's lives.

Through Mary's faith, the thirsty were quenched.

Through Mary's faith, the hosts at the wedding were saved from embarrassment.

Through Mary's faith, the servants at that wedding witnessed a miracle firsthand.

Others were comforted through Mary's faith. Through our faith in Christ, we can make a difference in other people's lives. Do we make life changes simply because it's better for those around us? Or do we seek to be closer to God, and the effects of our faith become a by-product of our acts?

As I write this, an April snow is falling in Minnesota. The birds are singing happily, despite the weather. Tina Samples, co-author of *Wounded Women of the Bible*, writes:

> What I do remember is being a lonely little girl, without a home, traveling to far-off places . . . While we traveled I sat on my mother's lap, learning to sing. In the midst of our family's problems and difficulties, my mother taught me to sing . . . She swept me up in her arms and pulled me close to her warm body. "Now listen," she would say before breaking into her deep alto. Beautiful music streamed from her lips. "Sing with me. You can do it!" Before long, I was singing the tune. I was only six at the time, but eventually learned to hold the melody while she danced around

it with harmony. In our sad little world, she found something worth singing about.[74]

There are people in this world that have the ability to comfort others in the midst of life's storms.

Where do they get this ability? What characteristics do they possess that empower them to give comfort to the less fortunate, to the wounded?

The Conductor tells a story of when he was about twelve years old. He was visiting with a neighbor girl in her front yard one day. They were talking about what was to come at church: confession. My husband says the neighbor girl had a little piece of paper in her hand. He reports she had written a list of all her sins so she would remember everything she needed to confess and have a clear conscience. She didn't want to forget any of them. (My adult husband drops his jaw and squints a Popeye-like eye as he recounts this story, clearly astonished by her desire to be right with God at age twelve). My twelve-year-old inquisitive future husband asked: "Can I read your list?" She did not allow such perusal, but she did ask if he had tallied a list himself. His response: he'd been outside playing. He was going to "wing it."

As charming as my husband was as a twelve-year-old, he now knows "winging it" is for kids. Once we are adults, and responsible for our own spiritual growth, if we are too busy doing other things and ignoring the spiritual aspect of our lives, "winging it" won't get us far.

---

[74] Dena Dyer and Tina Samples, *Wounded Women of the Bible* (Grand Rapids: Kregel, 2013), p. 9.

Our sin gets in the way.

We need to make our ways purposeful.

After Mary heard she would have a child, she traveled a great distance, on purpose, to visit her cousin Elizabeth, who was pregnant at the time with John the Baptist. There is comfort in being with others who understand what you are going through and who can strengthen and encourage you.

While with Elizabeth, Mary sang a song of praise:

My soul magnifies the Lord,
and my spirit rejoices in God my Savior,
for he has looked on the humble estate of his servant.
For behold, from now on all generations
will call me blessed;
for he who is mighty has done great things for me,
and holy is his name.
And his mercy is for those who fear him
from generation to generation.
He has shown strength with his arm;
he has scattered the proud in the thoughts
of their hearts;
he has brought down the mighty from their thrones
and exalted those of humble estate;
he has filled the hungry with good things,
and the rich he has sent away empty.
He has helped his servant Israel,
in remembrance of his mercy,
as he spoke to our fathers,
to Abraham and to his offspring forever.[75]

---

[75] Luke 1:46-55 (ESV)

Throughout this song, Mary is praising her God, rejoicing in his mercies, recognizing his blessings for those that are humble and glorifying her God for the great things he had done for her.

She was singing of his promises fulfilled and of what was yet to come.

Mary was doing what Jotham had modeled years before: "So Jotham became mighty, because he ordered his ways before the Lord his God."[76] One of those ways, in this moment, was giving praise and honor to whom it was due: God. She was saying yes to what was to come.

She walked near God.

The writer of Psalm 73 sings of God's wondrous qualities as well: "But as for me it is good to be near God; I have made the Lord God my refuge, that I may tell of all your works."[77]

And Mary was passionate about it.

I have a sister-in-law that is passionate about the Lord, too.

On Palm Sunday in 1997, my sister-in-law, a pastor, had preached the sermon that morning, entertained out-of-town guests with a large, home-cooked meal afterwards, all while experiencing a growing headache. After the meal, she excused herself, and left for her bedroom to lie down, hoping sleep would aid her pursuit of pain relief.

---

[76] 2 Chronicles 27:6 (ESV)
[77] Psalm 73:28 (ESV)

When she woke, her words were jumbled. Her husband, my brother, became concerned. He called his wife's doctor. They were advised to make an appointment the following day if the headache didn't go away.

It didn't sit well with my brother.

He called an Ear, Nose and Throat (ENT) doctor in his congregation. He asked my brother to give his wife the home phone extension so he could ask her a few questions. Once that part of the conversation was over, he instructed my brother to take his wife to the emergency room immediately. He would call ahead and tell the Emergency Room (ER) doctors what to look for.

The news was grim. She had a tumor on her brain. It had been there for years but had recently grown to the point that it was pressing on vital synapses. She was scheduled for surgery the next afternoon. Her chances of survival were not good.

My brother went home and informed his four small children their mother was sick. And prayed for a miracle.

The next day, when my brother arrived at the hospital, his highly educated wife did not know who the president of the United States was, evidently a common question to the confused. But she also didn't remember who her husband was, and had forgotten the four children who had suckled at her breasts.

There was no more time to wait. Her condition had deteriorated overnight. Surgery was moved up. It had become a life-or-death scenario.

As my sister-in-law was wheeled down the stark, sterile hospital corridor toward surgery, the normally mild-mannered, quiet woman warned in a raised voice, echoing for all to hear, "This better not take long. I have feet to wash!"

She had forgotten her husband, she had forgotten her children, but she hadn't forgotten her plans for the following Thursday—Maundy Thursday—to wash several people's feet in her congregation, just as Jesus did. She remembered the people God had called her to serve.

Despite your life's circumstances, despite the problems you are facing, do you remember there are others? Do you know who you should be serving?

I want to follow my sister-in-law's example and not focus on *my* problems of the day, but wave the proverbial fist in the air and yell, "This better not take long. I have feet to wash!"

In the words of author and missionary Elizabeth Elliot: "Leave it all in the Hands that were wounded for you."[78] When we stop trying to hang on tightly—often with clenched fists—to the things that God intends to take care of, our hands are free to be used for what *we* are intended to take care of.

Jesus was wounded. In that wounding, he died for you and for me.

---

[78] Daringdaughters.org; Elliott, Elizabeth.

Can we find a way to die, perhaps a little to ourselves, and help others despite our own wounds acquired from life?

In the first chapter of Luke, Mary responds to the Angel Gabriel's news that,

" . . . The Holy Spirit will come down to you, and God's power will come over you. So your child will be called the holy Son of God."[79] "Mary responded, 'I am the Lord's servant! Let it happen as you have said . . .'"[80]

We can learn a lot from Mary here.

I don't know about you, but when I am confronted with a new, daunting challenge in my life, my first reaction is *not* to humbly and quietly accept my new life's path. For many of my bigger challenges, I have cried, ranted, complained—and eaten—my way through to finally settling down and living with it. Mary's initial response is quite different. Her reply shows at least one of the reasons Mary is noted as "highly favored." She is obedient to her Lord's will. She is not *eventually* obedient. She does not *wait* to be obedient when it suits her. She is not obedient *after* she has tried it her own way first. She declares her obedience *while still in the midst* of her conversation with Gabriel.

I struggle here.

---

[79] Luke 1:35 Contemporary English Version (CEV) of the Bible
[80] Luke 1:38 (CEV)

163

When I feel God is directing me to do something, I first convince myself that I've heard wrong. Next, I talk myself out of it. And then I become miserable because I'm not doing what, deep down, I know I should be doing.

Mary skipped all of those very unnecessary, painful steps and faithfully responded affirmatively to her pending life change—for her *and* the rest of humanity.

She probably didn't understand the full implications of what that would mean, her son dying for all, but she responded positively regardless.

But isn't that what happens? We often look at the self-sacrifice and the work that will be involved in the act of obedience, yet have no clue how God will use our obedience in a much bigger way than we ever can imagine.

God will use your obedience in a much bigger way than you can ever imagine.

#SomeMiraclesNeedAMom | #AuthorSMcKeown

What opportunities are we missing to help others when we become embattled with our will to be obedient?

My husband's love language is touch (isn't that true for many guys?). He was adjusting our home's thermostat recently. I'm usually cold; he's usually warm. Finding a happy medium can be a challenge. As he walked away from the thermostat, I asked him what he had set it at. My quick-witted man declared, "It's set to 'snuggle.'" Meaning, he set it a little cooler than I like, so he can enjoy wrapping his arm around me while we sit on the couch and watch the news. If I'm too warm, it's not going to happen. My husband has set the stage for a certain outcome to occur: his love language need will be met, but I will also be loved in return.

Likewise, God has a plan as he puts things into motion in our lives.

We don't always understand, and too often we fight the position we find ourselves in rather than accept the process.

Joseph heard about the impending birth and planned to quietly back out of the wedding. After an angel explained things to Joseph, " . . . he did what the angel of the Lord had commanded him and took Mary home as his wife."[81]

Mary wasn't the only obedient person in this union. She married a man that had this quality as well.

Together, they lived obedient lives, doing what they believed was right in the eyes of God. After Joseph died, Mary continued on her path of obedience. Her faith gave others around her comfort, ease of pain, and help in times of trouble. Our God wants us obediently serving others.

And our world becomes better in that simple act.

---

[81] Matthew 1:24 (NIV)

For whoever does the will of my Father in heaven is my brother and sister and mother.[82]

Are you doing the will of your Father?

If you and I were sitting at the table with Mary in her kitchen today, what would she tell us? I think she would have wondrous stories of Jesus' life. She would tell us the incredible undocumented stories—what it was really like—when Jesus was growing up. Oh, how amazing it would be to hear such stories! But, I think she'd also lovingly run her hands over those worn spots of her scarred table, perhaps not even realize she was doing it, remembering her son who had once sat there, as she encouraged us to keep our focus on the Son of God. She would tell us to stay engaged with him *daily* as we go about our lives, to be imitators of him. When we are like Christ, we are ready to be used for greater purposes than ourselves.

"A woman in the crowd raised her voice and said to him, 'Blessed is the womb that bore you, and the breasts at which you nursed!' But he said, 'Blessed rather are those who hear the word of God and keep it!'[83]

And, just for the record, that neighbor girl my future husband talked to before church didn't want to forget her sins that day, but God does. When we ask for forgiveness, he forgives those sins. They're wiped clean.

That's how Mary lived. Wiped clean, righteous, humble, and passionate for God.

---

[82] Matthew 12:50 (ESV)
[83] Luke 11:27-28 (ESV)

And because she did, she quenched the thirst of those that were thirsty.

Do you know what God is asking you to do right now?

Who can you share that revelation with?

Are you ready to be accountable for that call?

Who can you ask to help you be accountable?

A simple prayer: *Dear Lord, help me to live like Mary: wiped clean, righteous, humble, and passionate for You.*

13

The Bridegroom, the Guests, and the Jar Fillers

I have shared our miraculous stories—especially that of our Determined one—with people that didn't know us during that season of our lives. It is of note that the more education people have, the more difficult it is for them to comprehend and believe the miracles I share with them.

Why is that?

Years ago, I was at a marketing conference when we were directed to split up into pairs with someone we didn't know and do an exercise. The purpose was to get us thinking about the individual projects we were considering marketing.

I turned around and found an introverted guy in a seat behind me. He was a gentleman and encouraged me to go first. I shared my first idea pertinent to the exercise. He nodded and agreed it was a great idea.

And then it was his turn. He stumbled. He hemmed and hawed. And he wasn't able to come up with an idea at that time. I tried to be encouraging, but we eventually sat down in our respective chairs to continue with the conference. It was at this point, after we had returned to our seats, the main presenter for the topic shared: "For those of you who are highly educated, you struggled with this exercise. Your brain isn't going to naturally bend this way."

Still wanting to be encouraging, I quickly turned around to my exercise partner. "Are you married?" (He'd already shared he was a college professor—a man who was highly educated). He looked confused but nodded. I continued: "Then today you have *two* women telling you what's wrong with you: you are too educated! That is why you couldn't come up with an answer." (I didn't speak of the obvious—that *I* was able to complete the exercise without a split second of difficulty!)

His seatmate immediately laughed out loud, appreciating my intended humor. The professor and I smiled at each other. But my point is, sometimes our reasoning gets in the way.

Other scholars have struggled with understanding miracles as well.

> . . . [Some scholars are] unwilling to take the words of Scripture at face value. They do not believe this was a miracle at all. They explain the story this way: There was a wedding, and they were running out of wine. Jesus told the servants to serve water when the wine ran

out. This was like a child's make-believe tea party. To try to play down the embarrassing situation, the head steward tastes the water that is served in place of the wine and says (in good humor), "Good wine!" Then, someone else at the celebration catches the spirit of the moment and adds, "Yes, this is the best wine yet!" I prefer to take John's account literally. This was a miracle. Jesus turned water—ceremonial, cleansing water—into the best wine men ever drank.[84]

The best wine. Ever.

Sometimes, however, reasoning isn't the problem.

The Bridegroom

Let's take a look at the bridegroom for a moment: he's the one with star-filled eyes at the festivities. He is likely beyond overjoyed that the day has arrived. But in this story, he is only briefly mentioned. " . . . Then he (the master of the banquet) called the bridegroom aside and said, "Everyone brings out the choice wine first and then the cheaper wine after the guests have had too much to drink; but you have saved the best till now."[85]

Did the bridegroom respond, rightly: "I had nothing to do with that decision." Or perhaps he merely saw this as another gift at the wedding?

---

[84] "The First Sign: Jesus Turns Water Into Wine," Robert L. (Bob) Deffinbaugh, bible.org.
[85] John 2:9c-10 (NIV)

Because, surely, arrangements had been made to serve the best wine at this celebration. Or, very likely, did the bridegroom quickly set it aside in his mind, not caring, because he had other things occupying it? This was his wedding! He'd waited for this week to arrive!

As stated in an earlier chapter, I was a wedding coordinator for several years. In the days I worked in that arena, if there was ever an organizational snag at a wedding, I *never* turned to the groom for a resolution. The bride, her family, and friends were usually the ones arranging details of the event. But in biblical times, that appears to be a different story. "The bridegroom generally procured some friend to order all things at the entertainment."[86]

If so, somebody's friend messed up!

Regardless, Jesus was at the wedding. He changed the water into wine. And people didn't know what to think.

The master of the banquet reports this magnificent tasting wine to the bridegroom. He possibly approached the bridegroom to ask where it came from, but certainly to ask why this great wine was brought out last. Regardless, I don't believe this bridegroom was overly concerned with the details and logistics of this wedding. They just weren't his focus. Again, he had his mind on what was happening on Earth that day; he most likely didn't have an eternal view at that moment in time.

And what about the guests?

---

[86] John Wesley, *Wesley's Notes on the Bible–New Testament*, 2017.

The Guests

As discussed in a previous chapter, some of the guests at the wedding *may* have been inebriated. I'm quite sure, though, that some were not. Purified drinking water wasn't readily available during Jesus' day. Wine was a safe, fermented drink. A built tolerance for the fermented drink would be, I believe, a side effect of the times. Those that were sober were most likely more aware of what was going on behind the scenes at the wedding, and quickly informed those less aware. It was just too exciting not to share.

I can only imagine how the buzz moved through those friends and family in attendance: "Did you hear? The ceremonial water was turned into wine. And it's the best wine ever, so they say. Apparently, Mary's son, Jesus, had a hand in it!"

It would be too unbelievable of a story. Perhaps they'd watched Jesus grow up in their community. He was just an ordinary boy, they would say. This just didn't make any sense. So, they'd possibly find another guest to question: "What have you heard?"

Isn't that what we do too often? Ask what others believe before we make our final decision to believe or not? Too often, we use our so-called "finger in the wind" to see which way the crowd is leaning.

And, of course, those older guests at the wedding, who know how a wedding *should* be done, are probably just focusing on how these young people just don't know how to do things these days: "We've never done it this way before!" It was unheard of to bring out the best wine after the guests had been drinking less-quality wine for days. The good stuff was brought out *first*, when taste buds could easily sample the excellence of the wine.

These guests were surely incredulous. How could they know what was being reported was true? Did they wonder if it was a joke? No one reported seeing Jesus do anything to convince him or her this was an actual miracle. If Jesus did a miracle, wouldn't he stand and make a dramatic statement? Wouldn't he call for everyone's attention, so they could see what he was doing?

How can this be? It doesn't make any sense? They must have had more wine out back!

We don't understand it. There was no wine and now there is plenty! And it tastes even better than the wine brought out earlier! Another guest must have brought this!

But they didn't see.

Jesus performed the miracle quietly. Again, it wasn't his time. This was a quiet, no fuss approach. And because of that, those not looking for a miracle didn't see it.

Just like us today. If we're not looking for a miracle, we don't see it.

The Gospel according to Matthew noticed Jesus' words about this as well: " ... Though seeing, they do not see. . ."[87]

The common cry: "Where is God?" is sometimes voiced when human need is displayed. God answered in this story, as he does many times, with a miracle. Too often, we just don't *see* it.

---

[87] Matthew 13:13b (NIV)

174

Likewise, many of the guests at the wedding in Cana never knew a miracle took place. They drank the wine but didn't know it was the result of a miracle.

How many miracles do we miss because we're not watching for them?

Jar Fillers

There were also the servants at this wedding. The jar fillers. These were the people who were directed to have a hand in the miracle.

As servants, jar fillers were accustomed to being obedient, to doing whatever they were told to do. It was their job. Mary directed them to do whatever Jesus told them to do, and I'm thinking, they may have questioned *among themselves* why. Perhaps they whispered: "Can you believe this? What is Jesus thinking?"

Imagine this: what if there was still some water leftover from the purpose of washing hands? The servants could have simply followed the directive of *fill them to the brim* without any need for emptying or cleaning out the vessels before doing the task. They could easily have been using water that had been previously used for an "unclean" task—washing hands. Ewwww! No thank you!

But they were obedient and did what they were told to do.

I believe their act of obedience changed them.

And God used their act of obedience for his purposes.

When we are obedient to God, he is in charge of the outcome.

#SomeMiraclesNeedAMom | #AuthorSMcKeown

The jar fillers were closer to the event than the bridegroom, the master of the banquet, or the guests. They actually *saw* the work required to pursue the miracle. They believed more readily than those that did not see the work.

In the view of an academic:

> I am thinking today of those presumably strong young servants who carried the stone jars and filled them with water . . . that those servants on the edge of the celebration were the only ones to actually witness the miracle here . . . it was the servants who saw this wondrous miracle of abundance play out right before their eyes. It was the servants who saw it all . . . they are the ones who went home with a story that night. They are the ones who first glimpsed the promise of Jesus. And so . . . they must have gone home with the dawning recognition that in the simple act of "saving" a party, the world itself was

about to change in Christ Jesus. Indeed, in Jesus the world itself was about to change.[88]

The jar fillers were trained to be obedient. They knew the value of compliance and were rewarded for that obedience with the knowledge of where the wine had come from. They knew it was a miracle.

The jar fillers' simple obedience increased their faith.

Simple obedience grows our faith.

#SomeMiraclesNeedAMom | #AuthorSMcKeown

Do we recognize a miracle when we see one? Or are we, like the bridegroom, too busy with other things on our minds? Or are we, like the guests, not really sure what just happened, debating it first to ascertain the direction of the crowd?

Guests at weddings are friends, obviously. We had friends in our lives that we revealed our struggles to. Most were sympathetic to our multitude of problems. Fewer recognized God's hand in the resulting miracles.

How can this be?

---

[88] Dancingwiththeword.com, "On Wine and Weddings" by Rev. Dr. Janet H. Hunt, January 13, 2013.

It doesn't make any sense?

Surely, the diagnosis was wrong!

The professionals that identified him with the disability clearly misdiagnosed him. They didn't know what they were doing.

A good friend once commented, "You could tell people to do all the things that you did for your kids, Sandy, but they wouldn't get the same outcome if they didn't have the God piece."

When your choice is drinking dirty water or tasting the best wine ever, what will you choose?

The master of ceremonies, not understanding where the new wine came from, is the man who, unwittingly, announces the miracle: "You have saved the best till last!"

The wine wouldn't have been there without the God piece.

Mary's son, Jesus, did it! Water was turned into wine!

I believe.

🌿

Are you a jar filler? Are you obedient and ready to do whatever our Lord tells you to do? I have no doubt you will see miracles when you take on this role. When you're willing to "do whatever he tells you," the Lord can make a way!

A simple prayer: *Dear Lord, help me to see Your ways and help me to become an obedient jar-filler.*

14

Taste it!

The guests drank the wine but didn't know it was the result of a miracle.

They didn't know.

How could they?

Those that weren't looking for a miracle didn't see one.

But the jar fillers *were* looking for a miracle. They wanted to know what the results would be. They were curious: did Jesus really change the water into a new wine?

If I had been behind the scenes at that wedding, filling those jars with water and nervously taking a cupful to the master of the banquet to be tasted, I would have been very interested to know what that wine smelled like, looked like, and tasted like.

According to wine enthusiasts, "Our taste buds detect sweet, sour, salty, and bitter. Sweet (residual sugar) and sour (acidity) are obviously important components of wine... There is no single formula for all wines, but there should always be balance between the flavors."[89]

The master of the banquet, the guests, and the jar fillers would know quality when they tasted it. I think the jar fillers would have been inquisitive—and maybe even tasted it, if they dared.

They were looking for a miracle.

The jar fillers' perspectives were changed that day.

They knew, firsthand, that Jesus of Nazareth, Mary's son, had extraordinary capabilities.

Mary had them, too.

Remember, it's possible—I believe probable—that Mary had experienced miracles within the meager four walls of her home before this day at the wedding. Why would she have gone to Jesus at the wedding if she didn't know he could do something about it? Why would she have told the servants to do whatever he told them to do? This miracle at Cana was Jesus' first *public* miracle. She already knew what he could do.

How did she know for sure? Because she had experienced the miracle of his virgin birth.

" ... Mary treasured up all these things, pondering them in her heart."[90]

There's no reason to believe Mary's character changed in those thirty years. I believe she reflected on the miracle at Cana, too.

We need to follow her lead. It's essential we learn to rejoice in the miracles, big and small, and hang onto them. Relish them.

---

[89] "How To Taste Wine," winemag.com 08-25-2015
[90] Luke 2:19 (ESV)

In verse nine of the account, the wine was tasted for the first time after the miracle. We need to "taste," or recognize, our miracles, as well.

It's good to taste the results of what God has done.

Sometimes it takes something extraordinary to happen for us to realize we aren't "tasting" as we should.

When I was eight and a half months pregnant with our surprise Princess, my husband was struggling with a decision. He had previously made a promise to me and his four sons that they would each get, in turn, a one-on-one trip, father and son, to wherever each son wanted to travel within the United States. This trip would occur in the summer when each son was approximately thirteen years old.

Our second son chose a train ride from the Midwest to California, exploring California, and then the train ride back home.

This trip had been planned for over a year. This pregnancy *wasn't* planned. But it was coming to fruition right about the same time as our Wanderer's trip. It took us a few months to get over the shock of discovering another child was on the way. Then, realizing the trip and birth were too close for comfort, the Conductor was torn about what to do. After discussing our options for a while, I told him I'd be fine. Go ahead and go on the trip. "If I happen to give birth while you're gone," I said, "I'll call and let you know what we had." No big deal, right?

The Conductor reluctantly agreed, but he formulated a secret plan before he left.

After he and the Wanderer left on their trip, I waddled around the house. I got my morning housework done and then settled in a chair in the living room to read.

The doorbell rang. It was a friend from church. In her hand she had a long-stemmed red rose. I was shocked! What was this? She didn't explain anything but delivered the rose with a smile and went on her way.

The next day, the doorbell rang again. And the next day. And the next.

My husband had arranged for eleven different ladies from our church to deliver a rose to me every day he was gone. I would receive a long-stemmed red rose, a friendly hug, a quick visit, and a "do you need anything" from each woman that my husband had sent.

On the twelfth day, my husband stopped at the floral shop and picked up the final rose and delivered it to me in person.

What a guy!

But I didn't really appreciate it in the moment. When he returned from the trip, we were just days from my due date. (My doctor had already said he wouldn't allow me to go over my due date with this pregnancy due to my age).

I had the Conductor's and Wanderer's twelve days of laundry to wash, meals to prepare, and the house ready to leave at the first hint of labor.

I was busy. Preoccupied. So focused on myself.

I forgot to stop and be truly thankful for what my husband had done.

A healthy Princess was born that July.

The following February, for Valentine's Day, our church hosted a banquet. One of the activities that occurred at this banquet was at each round table of eight people, we were directed to go around and share one story of something sweet that our husband had done. I shared this story about him having the roses delivered, one-by-one while he was out of town, and my husband and I were voted to stand before the crowd and share it with the other couples.

When it was my turn, and I shared this story with the crowd in the fellowship hall, our pastor reached for his white cloth dinner napkin and began waving it in surrender. The men all followed suit.

I was surprised by their collective reaction. What they seemed to be saying in their white flag solidarity was that the Conductor rose to the top of the crowd as an extraordinary husband.

I didn't fully realize it, or appreciate it, until that moment.

God, help us to remember to "taste" the good that is happening around us. To not just sloppily move on past the good things that are happening, but notice and appreciate them!

What else are we missing because we aren't focused on the good things that are happening in our lives? Or because it's not really a "big enough" miracle to fuss about?

What are we missing because we aren't focused on the good things that are happening?

#SomeMiraclesNeedAMom | #AuthorSMcKeown

Smaller Miracles Are Still Miracles

In the hills, near the Sea of Galilee, a crowd gathered around Jesus. He had compassion on them and fed the 4,000 who had gathered with seven loaves of bread and a few small fish. Sound familiar? Sure, it does. It happened near Bethsaida, as well, but that time Jesus fed 5,000 with five loaves and two fish. Which do you hear about more often, the feeding of 4,000 or the feeding of 5,000? I have to admit: I thought they were the same story for years. I had no clue they were two separate occasions. As a child in Sunday School, the story was always about the 5,000. Is feeding 4,000 any less of a miracle because we don't hear about it? It's still a miracle, right? The feeding of the 5,000 happens in Matthew 14:13. The feeding of 4,000 occurs in Matthew 15:29, the very next chapter.

Are we cynical enough to yawn a bored *ho-hum* because a bigger and better miracle has already occurred?

Small Miracles Count

Our Wanderer had trouble sleeping at night, fought depression, hated competition, and struggled socially. He scored pretty low on his college entrance exam—the first time. I needed to find a way to help him study to retake the test. I prayed, asking how I could help this son. And he reminded me that our Wanderer's interest in computers had exploded. So, I called the Area Education Agency to ask if they had a computer program to loan that would help my son study for the test.

They did.

I signed out the program, handed it to our Wanderer and walked away. What would be would be.

He scored a beautiful score the second time around and received almost a full scholarship at the school of his choice!

We had a few tough years with our Justice. When he graduated from high school and was in the car about to back out of our driveway a mere three days after graduating, he revealed to his father: "I'm never coming back here and if you happen to buy me Christmas gifts, you're just going to have to mail them."

My sarcastic husband lobbed back, "Well, don't make an announcement like that and disappoint us and show up."

And *that's* where we were at when he moved out of our house after two years of counseling.

But we continued to pray for our strong-willed son. He got involved with a really good church in his new city. And a few years later, for Mother's Day, he bought a card. He mailed it first to his brother in Maryland for that brother to sign. Then it was mailed it to his brother in Missouri for his signature. Then it was mailed to the oldest, in Minnesota, for his signature, and then it was transferred to their dad, who brought it home for our daughter to sign, back in Iowa. There was a lot of thought and effort put into this! And he also bought a plaque that read:

> My Mother
> Has given me the beauty of
> Family,
> The gift of
> Love,
> The comfort of
> Friendship,
> The guidance of
> Wisdom,
> The freedom of
> Truth,
> And the foundation of
> Faith.
> And I am eternally grateful.

It was a gift I will never forget!

A gift initiated by a son who feels deeply, but seldom shares it.

Our Determined son had the lowest possible expectations of all our kids from the professionals.

But God showed us, through prayer, each step we needed to guide our Determined through.

One particular small miracle that stands out in my mind with him was one day when he was waiting for his best friend to return a phone call. They were both in middle school at the time; they were at the age of learning social nuances. Our Determined was getting impatient to hear from his best friend, so he came to me and asked, "Would it be appropriate to call him instead of continuing to wait?"

Would it be appropriate? Where had he learned to ask *this* question? I was thrilled he was asking, especially since teaching social skills can be so difficult. He was learning!

Our first son, the Leader, who has had his own struggles but only occasionally needed parental assistance to maneuver through them, is also doing well. Another thing to be thankful for. We had enough battles to fight, didn't we? This son needed few things as a child and teenager, but has needed a few of the normal "stopgap" parenting helps as an adult. We lived only a few blocks apart.

We've got water spraying everywhere!

We're putting the house on the market—can you paint?

Can you babysit?

Dad, the car is making a funny noise.

I forgot my wallet.

187

These requests for help actually make us feel needed and loved. Who doesn't enjoy that? But we have also learned through helping our Leader that our kids all *want* different levels of assistance through their lives. What level is too much? What level is not enough? The Conductor and I follow our kids' leads.

Our only daughter, on who we have practiced our fiercest scare tactics with several boyfriends, is, at this writing, dating a man we *like*.

Is God not good?

We raised five kids to be independent, successful contributors to society, despite a myriad of diagnoses, a traveling husband, and the many weaknesses in our humanity as parents. With God, truly, all things are possible!

> I thank my God every time I remember you. In all my prayers for all of you, I always pray with joy because of your partnership in the gospel from the first day until now, being confident of this, that he who began a good work in you will carry it on to completion until the day of Christ Jesus. It is right for me to feel this way about all of you, since I have you in my heart and, whether I am in chains or defending, and confirming the gospel, all of you share in God's grace with me. God can testify, how I long for all of you with the affection of Christ Jesus. And this is my prayer: that your love may abound more and more in knowledge and depth of insight, so

that you may be able to discern what is best, and may be pure and blameless for the day of Christ, filled with the fruit of righteousness that comes through Jesus Christ—to the glory and praise of God."[91]

As a parent, I strived to be an obedient jar filler, one who knows I can do nothing without my Lord. When I'm obedient to him, *he* is in charge of the results.

One of our pastors of many years taught us, "God didn't expect us to do it all, but he did expect us to do something."[92]

Do something.

Don't just sit and watch the difficult things happen in life.

And then, watch for—and be thankful—for what God has done.

I led a small group of women from our church when we lived in Iowa through some character building, biblical studies. One day several of them were discussing the problems they were experiencing in their marriages. And it wasn't the first time. I remember slapping my hand down on the table, partly to stop the ill-tempered comments, partly to get their attention. I remember telling them, "Hold on! I'll be right back." And I walked down the hall to the lead pastor's office. I knocked on the door, and when he said, "Come in," I asked him if my small

---

[91] Philippians 1:3-11 (ESV)
[92] Pastor Tom Jacobs

group would do all the work to put on a marriage conference—and bring in a national speaker—if the church would foot the bill. He, rightfully, said he'd need to get back to me after bringing it before the church board, but he liked the idea.

The idea was approved and the conference was held. That first night we were serving a dessert during the break, and I didn't want any of my gals to miss the introductory sessions. I was in the kitchen alone cutting up store-bought cheesecakes for the coming break, crying while doing so. I was feeling all the feels in that moment. I was so excited about the possibilities of what God was going to do in the marriages of the people that were in attendance. And while I was crying, I was praying God would touch the hearts of those there. That they would learn more, do more than they ever thought possible because they were a little bit closer to a powerful Jesus because of this event.

I think Mary had the feels, too.

She acted on behalf of the people she loved. She expected good things to come from what the people had just learned: Jesus was more powerful than any of them understood. He performed miracles. He was the answer to their problems.

And the wine tasted exceptional.

Jesus did that.

Are you ready to give what you have and leave the outcome to Jesus? God wants to redeem your situation.

In this you rejoice, though now for a little while, if necessary, you have been grieved by various trials, so that the tested genuineness of your faith—more precious than gold that perishes though it is tested by fire—may be found to result in praise and glory and honor at the revelation of Jesus Christ. Though you have not seen him, you love him. Though you do not now see him, you believe in him and rejoice with joy that is inexpressible and filled with glory.[93]

What are you thankful for today? What have you not appreciated like you should have?

Is there something in your life that came to mind as you read this chapter that reminded you to actively rejoice with joy? What is it?

A simple prayer: *Dear Lord, please reveal to me what I need to be thankful for and what has been done for me and my family.*

---

[93] 1 Peter 1:6-8 (ESV)

15

Jesus Was Invited

Someone invited Jesus to the wedding. *Jesus and his disciples had also been invited to the wedding.*[94] Was he a friend? A relative? We don't really know.

Jesus was invited.

And because he was there, lives were changed.

At the very least, the hosts of the wedding were spared social embarrassment. At the most, the witnesses saw a miracle that changed their faith. They believed in Jesus.

What difference does it make to our children if we invite Jesus into our homes?

Everything. Because Jesus changes everything.

---

[94] John 2:2 (NIV)

When Jesus is invited into our homes,
it changes everything.

#SomeMiraclesNeedAMom | #AuthorSMcKeown

When my babies were first home from the hospital, I started singing to them. I sang a song that I learned in Sunday School when *I* was a child: *Jesus loves me this I know, for the Bible tells me so.* But instead of singing Jesus loves *me* throughout each chorus, I sang whichever baby's name I was holding, rocking, and comforting in the moment. I personalized it.

It was important for me.

They needed to hear right from the beginning of life that they were a child of God, and they were loved by him.

This was just the start of inviting Jesus into our home.

We also prayed. We read from children's Bibles. We occasionally even read children's devotionals together as a family. Like most families, though, we struggled with consistency. We had big age ranges— for a time—teens, toddlers, and tweens. Various learning disabilities and my own seemingly unending depression all contributed to a less than ideal family devotional time.

By inviting Jesus into our home, there was a calming confidence amid the chaos.

Believe me, we had plenty of chaos:

Screaming matches between siblings who struggled with communication.
Kids not answering a frantic mother's searching call due to very little communication.
An inquisitive preschooler climbing out on the roof.
A wandering child with the entire neighborhood searching for him . . . again.
A baby that didn't sleep through the night for three years.
Numerous ER visits due to sickness and falls.
Multiple fires started by a curious pre-teen.
Petulant, argumentative teenagers.
At times, a noise level at astounding decibels.
A husband who traveled extensively.
A mother fighting a long battle of depression.
Mountains of laundry.
Truckloads of groceries.
Mindless drudgery of another day to get through for a worn-out mom.

But in the midst of it all, miraculously, we had hope.

Truthfully, I never once questioned *if* we would make it through raising our five kids. But I had no clue what it would look like once our kids were all grown. Would we be visiting Determined in an institution as professionals predicted? Would *all* our kids be functioning in society independently? When they were young, and we were in the midst of so many battles, I couldn't envision what the future held for my babies.

When we invite Jesus into our home, there is a Light there. It guides us through all the dark storms that are raging. And we walk confidently through the storms because we aren't in the dark. There is a Light to guide us.

Where do we go to find this Light?

We start wherever we're at.

A simple, "Lord, are you there?" is a good place to begin.

And then ask for him to reveal himself.

I prayed for help in revealing my Lord to my children and their various personalities and learning challenges. I prayed he would be able to circumvent the communication difficulties *I* was dealing with on a daily basis with my kids and reveal himself to them in a way that they could each understand in their own learning style.

My Lord answered my prayers.

My husband and I were both present when each son prayed a simple prayer, asking Jesus into their hearts. I was at a committee meeting for church the night my husband was tucking our daughter into bed and she instigated the reception of the Lord. Our Princess, our sensitive child, prayed to receive Christ on the evening of September 11, 2001, one of those days on this Earth that felt like the whole world was in chaos. She sensed it even as a kindergartner.

When do kids start searching for God?

Do we, as parents, get out of the way and allow them to search?

Or do we allow our own pre-conceived ideas to influence our kids?

Do your adult eyes gloss over a Savior? Does your view of Christ hinder the views of your children?

" . . . but Jesus said, 'Let the little children come to me and do not hinder them, for to such belongs the kingdom of heaven.'"[95]

Teaching Truth

One of the things I happened to come across later in the parenting process is one of my favorite children's books, which I read to my kids (and now read to my grandkids). It's called *The Topsy-Turvy Kingdom* by Dottie and Josh McDowell. It's apologetics (the defense of Christianity) for kids:

> *Up is a word that I say when I look at a bird*
> *in a tree or the sky.*
> *Down is a place where I go when I fall from*
> *my bike or I slip on a pie.*
> *Hot is the water Mom runs in my bath; but*
> *cold is each splash on the floor.*
> *These are all things that I know to be true like*
> *I know two and two equals four.*[96]

---

[95] Matthew 19:14 (ESV)
[96] Dottie and Josh McDowell, *The Topsy-Turvy Kingdom* (Mexico: Tyndale For Kids, 1996), p. 1.

Two and two equals four. We learned this simple math equation at a very young age. Most rational people understand the concept of math and don't argue whether it's right or wrong.

But what's right and what's wrong *in life* are another matter.

"But what if the truth that you held in your heart would suddenly vanish away?
What if up became down, and cold became hot, and night was no different than day?"[97]

Moral and virtuous conduct in our nation has become muddied. We are a nation divided on what is right and what is wrong.

George Barna, founder of a market research firm that specializes in studying the religious beliefs and behaviors of Americans, writes:

> Christian morality is being ushered out of American social structures and off the cultural main stage, leaving a vacuum in its place—and the broader culture is attempting to fill the void. New research from Barna reveals growing concern about the moral condition of the nation, even as many American adults admit they are uncertain about how to determine right from wrong. So what do Americans believe? Is truth relative or absolute? And do Christians see

---

[97] Dottie and Josh McDowell, *The Topsy-Turvy Kingdom,* (Mexico: Tyndale For Kids, 1996), p. 2.

truth and morality in radically different ways from the broader public, or are they equally influenced by the growing tide of secularism and religious skepticism?[98]

As parents, my husband and I consciously, on purpose, daily and *passionately* taught our children right from wrong—not from the world's view but from God's view. We wanted them to understand that God's laws were good laws. They were made to help us make prudent decisions and live life wisely.

> *"The father was wise and was loved by most all. His kingdom abounded in joy.*
> *For he had made laws to protect everyone—every cat, every girl, every boy."*[99]

We tried to teach each of our children they were a loved child of God. There is a foundational faith that needs to be introduced to our children for them to grasp they are a child of God. They need this established in the home, because they won't hear it where God has not been invited.

> *" 'Perhaps Herbie's dad will never return,' a woman whispered in fear.*

---

[98] "The End of Absolutes: America's New Moral Code," barna.com, May 25, 2016

[99] Dottie and Josh McDowell, *The Topsy-Turvy Kingdom* (Mexico: Tyndale For Kids, 1996), p. 6.

'I don't remember there being a king,' yelled a foolish young man in the rear.'[100]

According to Barna, a large portion of society now believes this statement to be true: "Whatever is right for your life or works best for you is the only truth you can know."[101]

Barna also mentions that "finger in the wind" litmus test: "A sizable number of Americans see morality as a matter of cultural consensus. "[102] The problem with that litmus test is the wind is always changing.

My brother was riding a snowmobile in the midst of a winter blizzard when he was a teenager. He was trying to find his way through the storm, but the wind kept shifting. It wasn't a constant he could rely on to find his way in the blinding turmoil. He ended up digging a shelter in the snow and waiting out the storm in the shelter. He couldn't go forward; he couldn't go back. He was stuck in the storm because the winds kept shifting.

We need a constant to find our way.

And the only constant we have found is our God.

We taught our kids to think for themselves, to not go along with a changeable crowd. We tried to give them a foundation in the never-changing Word

---

[100] Dottie and Josh McDowell, *The Topsy-Turvy Kingdom*, (Mexico: Tyndale For Kids, 1996), p. 12.

[101] "The End of Absolutes: America's New Moral Code," barna. com, May 25, 2016.

[102] "The End of Absolutes: America's New Moral Code," barna. com, May 25, 2016.

of God on which to base their decision-making process.

We tried to teach them to follow Jesus, the God who was invited into our home—and, subsequently, introduced to our kids.

If we want a different outcome, it's imperative we introduce a different input. If we do things on our own—and their results are not ideal—why would we keep doing what we've done?

> *"And someone said, 'Truth is always the best—unless telling lies turns out better."*
> *And some said that stealing from others is wrong, except if you fancy their sweater."*[103]

Too many decisions have been based on doing what *feels* right in the moment. And then anything goes:

Thou *shall not* love thy neighbor.

Thou *shall* kill.

Thou *shall not* honor thy father and thy mother.

The freedom to make our own choices is ours, absolutely. As it is for our children, as well. Dr. Henry Cloud and Dr. John Townsend, co-authors of *Raising Great Kids,* state: "But to have a relationship requires two willing parties. You can't force your child to develop a relationship with God. God invites, but does not force himself. . ."[104] Cloud and

---

[103] Dottie and Josh McDowell, *The Topsy-Turvy Kingdom* (Mexico: Tyndale for Kids, 1996), p. 17.

[104] Dr. Henry Cloud and Dr. John Townsend, *Raising Great Kids* (Grand Rapids: Zondervan, 1999), p. 163.

Townsend add: " . . . you can *create a context that fosters connectedness to God* (italics theirs)."[105]

We see this concept demonstrated at Cana. Jesus offered more of himself at that wedding. He was willing to reveal who he was by the act of the miracle. It would be clear for those who chose to see: he was not just an ordinary man.

Of course, those that choose *not* to see often choose a life that is more complicated by those choices.

Or, in my "mothering" vernacular: "Go ahead and do that, but there will be consequences."

God has consequences, too. Whether we believe it or not, there *will* be consequences to our choices.

Sin has consequence.

"Like warm peanut butter, this rottenness spread till everyone took to the way
Of doing whatever they liked when they wanted, no matter what others might say."[106]

When we do whatever we want, doing whatever pleases us or seems right according to our feelings—or the crowd—we end up with a mess.

"But look at us now—the place is a wreck. Oh, why should there be so much pain?

---

[105] Dr. Henry Cloud and Dr. John Townsend, *Raising Great Kids* (Grand Rapids: Zondervan, 1999), pp. 163-164.
[106] Dottie and Josh McDowell, *The Topsy-Turvy Kingdom* (Mexico: Tyndale for Kids, 1996), p. 18.

I beg you, return to the ways of the king, for living like this is insane!"[107]

Too much pain.

We don't always admit we are living in a house of pain.

Zacchaeus wasn't afraid to admit it.

Biblical scholars teach that Zacchaeus ran ahead and climbed a tree to see Jesus: "And he was seeking to see who Jesus was."[108] Zacchaeus was a rich man, a tax collector, but he was also a thief.

When the opportunity arose, Zacchaeus wanted more. He wanted forgiveness, and he wanted Jesus.

"Those who sincerely desire a sight of Christ, like Zacchaeus, will break through opposition, and take pains to see him."[109]

And the opportunity arose.

He couldn't see Jesus from his vantage point, so he hurried to climb a tree. He wanted to see.

While seeking to see Jesus, he became seen. "And when Jesus came to the place, he looked up and said to him, 'Zacchaeus, hurry and come down, for I must stay at your house today.'"[110]

Jesus was a stranger to Zacchaeus. Zacchaeus didn't know him, but he had heard of him. There is a difference. Knowing Jesus and knowing of his existence is not the same.

---

[107] Dottie and Josh McDowell, *The Topsy-Turvy Kingdom* (Mexico: Tyndale For Kids, 1996), p. 20.

[108] Luke 19:3 (ESV)

[109] *Matthew Henry's Commentary* (Nashville: Thomas Nelson Publishers), Luke 19:1, p. 967.

[110] Luke 19:5 (ESV)

Regardless, " . . . he hurried and came down and received him joyfully."[111]

After Zacchaeus spent time with Jesus, he repented. He stood and confessed to the Lord that he had done wrong and promised to rectify those wrongs.

Are you looking for Jesus? Don't miss this opportunity. Because you are reading these words, the opportunity is now.

Forgive us, Lord, for being too busy, too lazy, too hard-hearted and lukewarm to run or climb to see you.

Some scholars believe Zacchaeus had some form of dwarfism and was looked on from society as someone with a disability. He wasn't highly valued in his town.

If so, Jesus didn't care about Zacchaeus' disability. He loved him just as he was. And Jesus' love changed Zacchaeus' standing. He called him out and showed his value to that crowd.

Do you have the passion to see Jesus?
Are you ready to invite him into your home?

C. S. Lewis writes of: " . . . the long terrible story of man trying to find something other than God which will make him happy."[112]

---

[111] Luke 19:6 (ESV)

[112] C. S. Lewis, *Mere Christianity,* https://www.dacc.edu/assets/pdfs/PCM/merechristianitylewis.pdf.

Are you done looking elsewhere, finding only a topsy-turvy world?

Remember, it isn't enough for our kids to believe in something because we, their parents, believe. They need to discover the truth for themselves; however, we need to be careful not to hinder that pursuit. If they don't believe, one appropriate response might be to say it's okay not to believe—for now. But what isn't okay is to stop looking.

Jesus loves them, this I know.
Little ones, to him belong . . .

Did you fail to invite Jesus into your home yesterday? It's not too late today.

A simple prayer: *Dear Jesus, I've been trying to do life without you. I realize now I can't. Forgive me. Please come into my life. Come into my home. Change me. Save me. I'm yours.*

If you prayed this prayer for the first time, salvation has come to *your* house today.

"By wisdom a house is built . . ."[113]

---

[113] Proverbs 24:3 (ESV)

16

Pursue the Solution

Here do you pursue a miracle?
Is it even possible?

And if you *do* attempt to go after a miracle, what are your chances of success?

It can seem daunting. But we, as parents and followers of Christ, can discover how to pursue miracles.

In the story at Cana, water was turned into wine; we've established that. It was a miracle! What was once mere water was transformed into the best wine ever. The master of the banquet declared it to be so.

But, I wonder. Water droplets in the form of rain fall onto grapevines regularly. Isn't that water turning grapes into wine? Is that agricultural phenomenon ever considered a miracle?

I sat next to a guy on a plane a few years back who worked for a vineyard. I asked him about the complicated process and what it was like to work for men who helped the miraculous progression every year. His tongue-in-cheek answer was, "Those guys believe they *are* God."

What *is* a miracle?

Merriam-Webster defines a miracle as, "an extraordinary event manifesting divine intervention in human affairs; an extremely outstanding or unusual event, thing, or accomplishment; a divinely natural phenomenon experienced humanly as the fulfillment of spiritual law. An unusual or wonderful event that is believed to be caused by the power of God; a very amazing or unusual event, thing, or achievement.[114]

An unusual event. Merriam-Webster believes miracles are unusual. My offhand response to this definition: Oh, Merriam-Webster, ye of little faith.

Job is one man who refutes that notion. (God) " . . . does great things and unsearchable, marvelous things without number."[115] The Bible states: "He performs wonders that cannot be fathomed, miracles that cannot be counted."[116] I believe they can't be counted because they are too numerous.

Jesus didn't just turn water into wine.

He healed the sick.

He raised people from the dead.

He calmed a storm.

He walked on water.

He fed thousands with a family portion.

He multiplied a catch of fish.

---

[114] George and Charles Merriam and Noah Webster, *Merriam - Webster Online* (Merriam - Webster.com) (Springfield: Merriam - Webster Incorporated, 2015).

[115] Job 5:9 (ESV)

[116] Job 5:9 (NIV)

He provided the funds for taxes in the mouth of a fish.

The Bible provides the details of thirty-seven miracles performed by Jesus. But those are just the ones mentioned in the texts.

Most of the miracles mentioned seemed effortless on Jesus' behalf. He spoke the words, and the tree withered.[117] He told a man to walk, and the man walked.[118] He commanded a dead man to rise, and the dead man rose.[119] From the outside looking in, these events occurred quite effortlessly.

I believe a seemingly *effortless* miracle is more often recognized as a miracle. Its occurrence appears rare, just as Jesus' effortless miracles were in biblical times. Hear me. I am not saying miracles are rare. What I am saying is that miracles that don't require human effort seem to be more rare.

When our friends' children were young, they left them at their maternal grandparents' farm in Texas to be babysat while they went on a date to see a movie. While the parents were relaxing inside the cinema complex, a tornado developed, touched down, and was barreling toward the old farmhouse . . . and their children.

The winds roared. The black clouds swirled. Texas dirt flew. And the thin walls of the aged house started to ripple as the tornado neared. Their young son, standing in his grandparents' living room, stretched out his hand and declared, "You cannot come here."

---

[117] Matthew 21:19 (ESV)

[118] John 5:8 (ESV)

[119] John 11:43-44 (ESV)

And the buckling of the walls ceased.

When the parents emerged from the movie theater, they heard the tornado warning signals blaring throughout the area and rushed to their young children. As they approached the grandparents' home, they saw a tornado path leading directly to the old farmhouse. But as they drove closer to the structure, they saw that the path split, evidence of the twister going around the house on both sides, and then merging once again after rounding the house.

It was a miracle!

But hear me: those inside the house saw the walls stop rippling. They heard the wind cease. They saw the skies clear through the windows. But that was all they knew from their immediate vantage point.

When the parents climbed a hill overlooking the farm and saw the path split before the house and converge into one massive, wider flattened route on the other side, they had no doubt: a miracle had occurred!

If you only heard the story that the tornado didn't hit the house, what would you presume?

The tornado missed the house.

It turned at just the right moment.

They were so lucky.

But that wasn't what happened.

Their son stretched out his arm, spoke the words, and the tornado split in two. A miracle occurred. It was instantaneous.

And that's not the whole story.

This boy was only three years old at the time. Three. Years. Old.

Think about this! A three-year-old boy declared authority over a powerful twister. If you are reading these words, you, too, are capable of pursing a miracle.

If a young boy has enough faith—enough authority—to pursue a miracle, how can *we* not?

Having the faith of a child is, indeed, a necessity, but what else is needed?

At the wedding in Cana, the writer didn't take note of Jesus speaking words of command, or putting his hand up to facilitate the miracle. John noted Jesus asked for participation in this miracle. He asked for participation, but *Jesus* had all the power. The miracle happened because Jesus was there, not because the servants were. He asked the servants to fill the jars and then to pour them out. There was an activity involved in this miracle. Jesus asked, and the servants went to work.

When a problem is discovered, you attempt to understand the problem to the best of your ability. If you come to the realization that there is no earthly way you can solve the problem, the next step is to pursue a holy solution: a miracle.

Have *you* tapped into a powerful God?

#SomeMiraclesNeedAMom | #AuthorSMcKeown

When our family was amassing difficulties, we recognized the strain we were under. My brother and his wife, both pastors, told us years later they were worried our marriage wouldn't survive the many struggles we were facing.

We were no longer willing to live in those circumstances. It was time to fight for a different life.

These are the resources our family used to pursue our miracles for our family. I encourage your family to engage them, as well.

One: **Faith.**

We needed to *believe* it was possible.

"And whatever you ask in prayer, you will receive, if you have faith."[120]

Educating ourselves, reading to understand what issues we were dealing with, was just part of it. Once we recognized the problems, we needed to stand and fight them in faith.

Part of increasing our faith involved going to church. Every Sunday.

I know attending church every Sunday may seem a bit "old fashioned." I could quote you statistics from Gallup or the Pew Research Council, but they'd have changed by the time this is printed. Attending church has always been a necessity for sanity. It has grounded us. It has given us direction. And hear this: we didn't wake up on Sunday morning and *decide* if we were going to church or not that day. We decided on the Sunday before that we were going the following

---

[120] Matthew 21:22 (ESV)

Sunday. And we planned for it throughout the week. We got our grocery shopping done, our laundry done, and our play time done on other days of the week so we could go to church on Sunday.

One of the things I looked forward to in church was having no kids at my side for the hour I was in the service. It was usually the only hour in the 168 hours of the week that I had without a kid at my side or sleeping in my bed (that's another story). But another benefit for me was an hour of hearing a message filled with hope. I've spoken with the man who pastored the church during those years, reminding him of something he said that was so encouraging. I held onto this for a long time, and still do today. He said, "I am convinced God somehow changed my words in mid-air, using them to encourage others with words that were his, not mine."

Of course, one hour of church on Sunday does not fill our souls enough to last for the next 168 hours. We need more Son energy than that!

It was during these years I learned to cling to, and read, the Word of God for comfort. As I read, my faith grew. Oswald Chambers writes in *My Utmost For His Highest*: "When we truly live in "the secret place," it becomes impossible for us to doubt God. We become more sure of Him than of anyone or anything else."[121]

And I read amazing stories. "And God was doing extraordinary miracles by the hands of Paul . . ."[122] If

[121] Oswald Chambers, *My Utmost For His Highest* (Grand Rapids: Discovery House Publishers, 1992), August 23.
[122] Acts 19:11 (ESV)

God could do extraordinary miracles through Paul, why not through our family?

As I continued to read, I learned to value my faith. "And he did not do many miracles there because of their lack of faith."[123]

Without faith, there would be no miracles.

Two: **Focus**.

What's on your to-do list for today? Does it include "pursue a miracle"?

We are encouraged to " . . . drink the cup . . . "[124] To do the hard things in life.

The servants were focused when they were performing their task.

If you are on social media in any form, you have probably read a rant about poor service. Can you imagine these servants being self-absorbed in other tasks?

Excuse us; we were in the middle of a dice game out back. Messing with those jars is a lot of work, and that's just going to have to wait a bit.

There is a focus required to get results.

When Determined was first diagnosed with autism, I called our pastor and resigned from all of the volunteer work I was doing at church. It turned out I was on seven committees. I heard him later joke, "I delivered Sandy McKeown from seven committees this week!" I had no clue I was on that many church committees. How do things creep up on us like that? For me, I was often so flattered that I was asked, I

---

[123] Matthew 13:58 (NIV)
[124] John 18:11 (ESV)

never even considered saying no. I had to learn that word. N-o. And use it.

Part of focus is being selfless. My husband is a selfless man.

I've written, previously, of the Conductor stating his children were his hobby. That's how he lived during those years of struggles. He put down his golf clubs and played with his kids. His involvement with our kids will affect our family for generations to come. Of that, I have no doubt.

Three: **Forgiveness**.

A clean heart is needed.

"And when he saw their faith, he said, "Man, your sins are forgiven you.""[125]

Cleaning out the vessels needed to be done.

My relationship with my mother was not an easy one. When the stressors of these life events cropped up, I had even less patience for a strained relationship. But I discovered *she* had had some serious difficulties of her own growing up. She did the best that she could at that time. It was in my best interest to forgive her. We need to clean out the vessels in our own lives to make room for the blessings.

> What steps are you ready to take to pursue a miracle for your family?

Four: **Friends** and **Family**.

I discussed this already in chapter 5, "Mary Had People," so I'll just briefly touch on it here. Our

---

[125] Luke 5:20 (ESV)

friends and family were invaluable to us in the trying years. When we didn't know the right people, our friends and family were able to refer us. You just can't do life alone if you want to pursue a miracle.

Five: **Flexibility**.

I found I had the tenacity to do the work, but we needed to adjust how we did things.

We couldn't adhere to "this is the way we've always done it" to get through the seasons of difficulty. My husband reduced his travel for work. We took a significant pay cut, but we survived as a family. Our family was worth it. I needed the extra support during that time.

When we first discovered Determined was autistic, that these problems we were experiencing with him were not going to go away overnight—that this would, possibly, be a lifelong battle—strategies needed to be adjusted.

After the initial crisis was over, we needed to work on getting back on track with several things. One of those things: our marriage. Yes, we were still together, but we needed some reconnecting. We dropped our kids off in three different states (no one household was too excited to take the collective crew!) and we went away to a marriage retreat. It felt so strange to be without the kids. After a few hours of driving, my husband turned around and yelled to the back of the van, "Sit down and quit your fighting!" I looked at him like he'd lost his mind. He quipped with a twinkle in his eye, "I don't want to get out of practice."

Six: **Fearlessness**.

Doing the hard things when you're fearful is part of adulting, right? Don't let fear stop you! This was discussed in chapter 6, "Sometimes You Do It Afraid."

"He said to them, 'Why are you so afraid? Have you still no faith?'"[126]

He said to them, in essence: *Where is your faith?* " . . . And they were afraid, and they marveled, saying to one another, 'Who then is this, that he commands even winds and water, and they obey him?'"[127]

We never contemplated *not* making it through the tough times. Did we know what it would look like on the other side of the season? Absolutely not. But we did know we would somehow, some way, make it through.

One of the reasons why we knew we would make it through is because we worked at it. Every. Single. Day. We didn't decide one day we weren't going to keep working on these things any more. We worked on Determined's physical therapy. We worked on speech therapy with the Wanderer, Justice, and Determined. We worked on helping Wanderer's moods and on developing good sleeping habits for him. We worked on Justice's interpersonal relationships with his siblings.

---

[126] Mark 4:40 (ESV)
[127] Luke 8:25 (ESV)

Seven: **Father God**.

What's your relationship with your heavenly Father like?

Oswald Chambers, author of *My Utmost for His Highest*, writes: "Get to the end of yourself where you can do nothing, but where He does everything."[128]

When we realize we can do *nothing* without him, we're in a good place. When we focus on earthly things, it clouds everything else. When we focus on God, everything else becomes clear.

"As for me, I would seek God, and to God would I commit my cause, who does great things and unsearchable, marvelous things without number ..."[129]

Are you *ready* to pursue a miracle?

What's the next step you need to take to pursue a miracle for you and your family?

If you don't know the answer to these questions, ask God for the direction you need: *Dear Lord, help me. I am unsure what to do next. Please show me the way.*

Self-assessment

Circle the item(s) listed below you need to pursue your miracle. Do you have:

Faith?

Focus?

---

[128] Oswald Chambers, *My Utmost For His Highest* (Grand Rapids: Discovery House Publishers, 1992) August 22.
[129] Job 5:8-9 (ESV)

Forgiveness?
Friends and Family?
Flexibility?
Fearlessness?
Father God?
If you're missing components on this list, pray for direction. Start with this simple prayer: *Dear Lord, increase (my) faith!*[130]

---

[130] Luke 17:5b (ESV)

17

Would the Miracle Have Happened without Mary?

What if Mary wasn't at the wedding?

I can only assume Mary was active in her community. If so, it would be quite natural for her to miss a fun, much-anticipated neighborhood or family event. She could have chosen to be "pouring out," to ignore what she had originally planned and taken care of a sick friend, perhaps. What if something like this had occurred?

Would the miracle have happened without Mary in attendance at the wedding?

I don't believe so.

I believe some people are born "for such a time as this." And this was part of what Mary was supposed to do in her time.

Who but Mary would have known what Jesus could do?

Who but Mary had such a close relationship with her son, the Son of God?

Who but Mary knew to direct the servants with absolute confidence to do whatever Jesus said to do?

Mary recognized there was no more wine and knew what he could do. She knew he performed miracles.

And she pursued one.

It's Mary's urging for Jesus to act that sets the miracle into motion.

Yet, Mary didn't stand prominently and watch, making sure things were done just right.

Mary knew it wasn't about her. This was something Jesus had to do.

After all, it was about Jesus.

It's always been about Jesus.

In the Gospel of John, we don't see Mary again until she is at the foot of the cross, where she witnesses her son's horrific, torturous death by the hands of the neighbors she is commanded to love.

She was part of Jesus' joyous and miraculous birth, she initiated his first public miraculous sign, and she watched, her heart shredded in unbelievable pain, as he demonstrated his miraculous love for all of us—a love so deep that he took on our sinners' punishment.

The Gospel of John is considered by many scholars to be the Book of Signs. In my simple understanding, a sign gives us direction. It's not a destination.

Imagine a fabulous vacation spot you've heard from friends is the best place they've ever been. Now you and your family are on the way to this wonderful destination for the first time. As you travel, along the side of the road, you see a sign on the shoulder giving you directions on how to get to your intended destination.

Do you stop at the sign? Do you stay there, expecting and hoping for the experience you're seeking?

Why would you?

That sign isn't your destination.

Likewise, we don't stop on our journey because we have experienced miracles. They are only signs, pointing us to Jesus.

There's more to this journey.

"This, the first of his signs, Jesus did at Cana in Galilee, and manifested his glory. And his disciples believed in him."[131]

These signs point us to Jesus. They strengthen our faith.

Mary had already seen signs in her own home, where the Son of Man lived. And his disciples also saw miracles not written about in the Bible. "Now Jesus did many other signs in the presence of his disciples, which are not written in this book; but these are written so that you may believe that Jesus is the Christ, the Son of God, and that by believing you may have life in his name."[132]

---

[131] John 2:11 (ESV)
[132] John 20:30-31 (ESV)

Signs point us back to Jesus, so we may believe. They help us to see the Savior in our midst.

The signs in the Bible " … revealed Jesus' glory … "[133]

The wilderness and the dry land shall be glad;
the desert shall rejoice and blossom like the crocus;
it shall blossom abundantly
and rejoice with joy and singing.
The glory of Lebanon shall be given to it,
the majesty of Carmel and Sharon.
They shall see the glory of the Lord,
the majesty of our God.[134]

They. Shall. See.

It's not just a miracle that we see a miracle. It's a miracle when we see, and recognize, the glory of the Lord.

But once we're at Jesus' feet, what do we do?

Eric Metaxas wrote, "Being a Christian is less about cautiously avoiding sin than about courageously and actively doing God's will."[135]

Mary was the epitome of courageously doing God's will:

- Discovering she was somehow, unfathomably, expecting a child while yet an unmarried

---

[133] John 2:11 *The NIV Study Bible*, Study Notes (Grand Rapids: Zondervan, 1995).
[134] Isaiah 35:1-2 (ESV)
[135] ericmetaxas.com, June 10, 2014 blog entry

woman who had never lain with a man.[136] Finding herself in a tough spot socially, but carrying on with grace and dignity.

- Mercifully, the man of great character that was to be her husband didn't abandon her after hearing of the surprise impending birth, even though he'd planned to initially. He took the high road and married her. She didn't retaliate that initial rejection with a hurting, emotional rejection of her own but received him.[137]

- Traveling over primitive, unsafe roads while nine months pregnant to obey the laws of the land for a census.[138]

- Giving birth in a stable.[139]

- Fleeing in the middle of the night to save the life of her young son from a vengeful dictator. [140]

- Experiencing mixed feelings of fear and pride as Simeon spoke prophetic words over her son and his purpose on this earth.[141]

- Searching desperately for her missing son who stayed behind to teach wisdom beyond his years: "Why have you treated us so?"[142]

---

[136] Matthew 1:18 (ESV)
[137] Matthew 1:24 (ESV)
[138] Luke 2:3-5 (ESV)
[139] Luke 2:7 (ESV)
[140] Matthew 2:14 (ESV)
[141] Luke 2:34 (ESV)
[142] Luke 2:48 (ESV)

- Getting jostled in a large unruly crowd, unable to even get close enough to her son to see him.[143]

Mary was a Steel Magnolia, a woman amazingly strong of character, a woman with uncommon fortitude.

Her role as the mother of Jesus was not easy, but she grew in her faith through the difficulties she endured.

These experiences in life prepared her for more of what God had planned for her to do.

At the wedding in Cana, she was destined to stand in the gap and fight for a miracle for the people she loved. She had the faith within her to do so.

God's Word teaches us about being able to do extraordinary things when we acquire big faith:

Believe me that I am in the Father and the Father is in me, or else believe on account of the works themselves. Truly, truly, I say to you, whoever believes in me will also do the works that I do; and greater works than these will he do, because I am going to the Father. Whatever you ask in my name, this I will do, that the Father may be glorified in the Son. If you ask me anything in my name, and I will do it.[144]

---

[143] Luke 8:19 (ESV)
[144] John 14:11-14 (ESV)

Who else at the wedding knew they could ask for anything in Jesus' name, and he would do it?

Who else could have stepped into Mary's spot and pursued a miracle?

The bridegroom?

The bride? (There is no mention of her, but certainly where there is a groom ...)

The master of the banquet?

The servants?

The guests?

Who there had the faith of a mother who had been through what Mary had been through? Who knew that whatever she asked in Jesus' name, he would do?

There was no one else.

It was Mary's purpose to act.

If Mary hadn't been there, the wedding would have been a social disaster, for sure.

Whose faith would never have been formed because of what didn't occur?

The newlyweds would never recall the wonders that had occurred at their wedding. The master of the banquet who tasted the best wine ever would never have announced, albeit most likely unknowingly, the first public miracle ever. The servants would probably never witness or be a part of a miracle in their lifetime. And the guests probably would have gone home early, disappointed and disgruntled due to lack of refreshments at the wedding.

So, what's the big deal? None of these alternate scenarios are earth-shattering. Everyone could live with these different scenarios.

But it changed the way people saw Jesus.

He thus revealed his glory, and his disciples put their faith in him.

And faith started growing.

That's the difference.

Miracles cause faith to grow.

#SomeMiraclesNeedAMom | #AuthorSMcKeown

When we pursue Jesus today, we do so by praying and reading his Word. When we read that Word, we drink his water.

"Jesus said to them, 'I am the bread of life; whoever comes to me shall not hunger, and whoever believes in me shall never thirst.'"[145]

In my own family, who would have researched the learning styles, read countless books on raising challenging children, kept track of three IEPs, attended regular staffings, driven three different kids to speech therapy, and worked countless hours on physical therapy at home. Doing it over and over and over again. Because, to get our miracles, the required obedience—the required faith—was cumulative.

[145] John 6:35 ESV

Remember, these ideas didn't come from within; they were inspired by an all-knowing Lord. He knew what was needed to accomplish the miracles.

It started in that comfy chair the day the leaf unfurled behind me years before. I learned how to listen to God. And then I learned to obey.

And then I learned:

Some miracles need a mom.

Mary knew.

Are you inspired by ideas from the Lord?

If not, pray and ask for those ideas.

A simple prayer: *Dear Lord, I need Your wisdom to know what to do for my family. Please show me what to do.*

18

When Your Miracle Isn't Happening

After a few months away at college, our boys called home, often astonished at some of the things they were learning their freshman year. Most of the time it was things *outside* of the classroom that surprised them.

Determined and Justice had the shortest amount of patience growing up. I would often buy a case of SpaghettiOs for quick meals in between the various activities on the household agenda. It was my economical replacement to drive-thru pit stops for our large family.

But SpaghettiOs weren't quite fast enough for our impatient ones.

Grabbing the can out of the pantry, searching for the can opener in the drawer, opening the can, thwacking the contents of the can into individual microwave-safe bowls, and then placing the too-hot bowls in the freezer to cool off while my kids screamed impatiently just became tedious. One day, I decided to skip a step. I decided these SpaghettiOs were already pre-cooked, so why did I need to heat them up?

I began pouring those SpaghettiOs into their bowls and sliding them across the table with the speed and precision an experienced server would be proud of. And I did this for years. When they got older and could operate a can opener themselves, I failed to mention that heating them up would be a normal thing to do.

They were fine with the process. They didn't complain about it at all. Why mess with it?

Until I got the phone calls from college. "Did you know everyone else on the planet heats up the SpaghettiOs first, Mom?" they asked incredulously. They were a little miffed I had given them food right out of a can without the proper preparations. They had discovered this anomaly when their college roommates watched their process in the shared dorms—horrified, of course.

We still have a good laugh about that one.

At least we can laugh. I'm very thankful for that laughter.

Sometimes, decisions we make hurt too much and laughter is not a part of the equation.

In an interview, Dolly Parton shared how people were telling her she needed to talk to her famous goddaughter. This goddaughter's recent actions seemed to be demonstrating character that was different than what some of her life goals would require—things this person might later regret. Dolly had some wisdom for her friends: "Everybody's different. You've got your own journey. And some people are going to help you along the way, and they can kick a few rocks out of the road for you, but you got to walk it."[146]

Everybody's different. I couldn't agree more.

And sometimes, someone else's journey may feel like its trampling all over your own.

One of our sons has never wanted help along the way. He didn't want us to kick a few rocks out of the road for him. He wanted to walk his own walk. He wanted to make his own mistakes; this he made very clear.

This son has been different from the get-go. I'm speaking of our Wanderer. He started forging his own paths when he was four years old, and he hasn't stopped yet—as far as we know.

We haven't seen him for eight years at this writing.

We believe he has just three kids. We've never laid eyes on the third one.

The Conductor and I did something that made him angry. We can only speculate on what *really* made him mad, because it's never been communicated to us. It has been a long eight years without him and his family.

It hurts.

When we are hampered by the unknown, we cling to the known.

---

[146] Andy Sahadeo, "Dolly Speaks About Goddaughter Miley Cyrus: 'Miley has such gifts.'" Foxnews.com, Nov. 20, 2019.

And this I know. Even though I don't understand the specifics, I believe I know the "who":

In the movie *Hook*, Dustin Hoffman plays the main character. After kidnapping Peter Pan's children from his new life, Hook puts great effort into teaching Peter's children that their parents do not love them. He establishes a classroom. He requires them to sit at desks. And with much assurance, he points out all of the human failings of the parents to these innocent children, as he leans close and whispers his lies. He doesn't allow them to recall the good things their parents did.

I have absolute certainty Satan has told our Wanderer lies. He has reminded our son of all our human failures and convinced him with his lies that we do not love him.

We absolutely *do* have human failures—numerous failures! But he is dead wrong when he tells our son that we don't love him!

I don't think we can be a parent without being misunderstood by our kids. They don't have the maturity to understand and appreciate what we do.

It is our prayer that someday our Wanderer will remember how much we love him.

Mary's son, Jesus, distanced himself from her, as well. Jesus responded to Mary about the lack of wine at Cana: " . . . Woman, what does this have to do with me? My hour has not yet come."[147] Scholars point out: "The title 'woman,' . . . seems to be used to establish *distance* between Jesus and the other party."[148]

---

[147] John 2:4 (ESV)

[148] Eric D. Svendsen, *Who Is My Mother*, (Amityville: Calvary Press, 2001), p. 183.

But it didn't deter Mary. She continued to do what she thought should be done. In this case, pursue a miracle for people that needed one.

Help us, Lord, to not be deterred!

We pray for our distant son and his family every day. My husband even prays that they will someday be at our family events. But, for some time, I couldn't even hope for that.

Our hurt has given us compassion for others with similar hurts. One couple we know had a family member cut them off because they were following "boundary" teachings. Dr. Henry Cloud, one of the authors of *Boundaries*, writes:

> In talking with some people who have read the book, we've realized that a few have selfishly misused the point, which is to make relationships better. Instead, these people have tried to use boundaries to control other people or to make a big deal out of very small issues. So understand what we mean when we say you are to avoid toxic people: Imperfect behavior is not the same as toxic behavior. It's important to learn the difference between problems that we should expect in relationships because people are imperfect, and problems that are toxic and need to be worked through or else avoided . . . There is no reason to start a war over someone's immaturity or perfections that rub us the wrong way. That is the time for us to grow

in patience and longsuffering, the ability to wait on people as they grow and mature. . . We all have to learn to be patient with one another's imperfections and flaws, and to give each other time to grow."[149]

Waiting to grow our own patience and longsuffering isn't easy.

Autism, oppositional defiance, years of sleepless nights, depression that came again and again—these were not our biggest giants, our most difficult challenges. We dealt with all of those problems head on and fiercely. But with this challenge, we believe God is telling us to be still and be quiet.

Why do you fight and argue with each other? Isn't it because you are full of selfish desires that fight to control your body? You want something you don't have, and you will do anything to get it. You will even kill! But you still cannot get what you want, and you won't get it by fighting and arguing. You should pray for it. Yet even when you do pray, your prayers are not answered, because you pray just for selfish reasons.[150]

We love our son! Is that selfish? I don't think our love is selfish, but perhaps the way we showed our love was.

---

[149] Dr. Henry Cloud, www.boundaries.me, June 8, 2020.
[150] James 4:1-3 Contemporary English Version (CEV) of the Bible

Love is not just a feeling—it's an action word. It doesn't feel right to say or do nothing! But unless the Lord tells us otherwise, we will obey . . . and wait.

Last summer I was mourning this child at a deeper level than I had ever done before. A pastor had referred another mom to me that was going through a similar experience. (The number of adult kids not speaking to their parents in this day and age is staggering). I don't know if helping this mom triggered some feelings I hadn't dealt with, but I could not stop crying.

I finally called a good friend that is a retired social worker. In between tears I told her I was crying constantly and couldn't stop thinking about our Wanderer.

And she gave me some good advice. She said: "Sandy, you have really good coping skills. If you are still crying this much despite your good coping skills, it's probably time to go talk to someone."

So I did. Go talk to someone. And this counselor, after getting the gist of my story and getting to know me a little bit, said: "You've stopped hoping." And then she admonished me: "You can't give up hope on your child."

But I had a sick heart.

"Hope deferred makes the heart sick . . ."[151]

I had already hoped, and prayed, but I still wasn't seeing our son.

This is our son who has a 1,000-watt smile with a naturally mischievous personality. He's so much like his dad!

---

[151] Proverbs 13:12a (ESV)

This is our son who tested highest on the pre-college exams of all our kids and is so good with computers.

This is our son who has a gift of writing.

This is our son who loves animals.

This is our son who loves movies, horseback riding, and being a stand-alone guy.

This is the son I miss terribly.

But I haven't seen, or spoken to him, for eight years. I wonder what new interests he's developed. Is he a good husband? Is he a good father? If he's anything like his dad, he is.

To work on healing my heart, I needed to stop focusing on what I *didn't* have, and focus on what I *did* have. Being thankful is good for the soul.

When I realized over the years that I don't have any control over the outcome of our relationship with this son, these are the things that have helped me.

First, I watched those who have had it much harder that we have. And, hey, there is *always* someone who has had it harder than we do.

The Conductor and I met a couple almost forty years ago that would become lifelong, worthy-to-be-followed friends.

I ended up in the crying room with our firstborn on our first visit to a new church in a new city. Inside was a friendly lady with a baby about the same age as mine. They had tried for years to have a second child but were unable to, she informed me. Through adoption, this child was the answer to their prayers.

We became fast friends, and, through the years, this couple always loved, always cared. They would babysit when we had no money to pay a sitter. They hosted our kids and me when my husband was out of town for work on Thanksgiving and Christmas. A nurse, my new friend was my back-up coach for unpredictable labor and deliveries. She called daily to check up on me when she knew I was struggling while my husband traveled.

And, through this entire relationship, we watched as the boy who was the answer to their prayers grew from innocent childhood to mischievous pre-teen. Their son was later diagnosed with a mental illness and became truly troubled.

We watched this couple pray as their son became hooked on drugs.

We watched this couple pray as their son began stealing to purchase the drugs.

We watched our friends pray as they visited their son in jail.

We watched as they prayed for a job for their once-incarcerated son.

We watched as they prayed for their son's girlfriend's pregnancy.

We watched as they prayed—and selflessly took care of—their son's first child . . . and second child . . . and third.

And we watched as the judge took the children away, they were adopted out-of-state, and the grandparents said their goodbyes.

With another move, our visits lessened, but last summer they arrived for a quick stopover. After their overnight stay, we were walking them through the garage entrance, when my friend turned to her husband and proclaimed, "Wait a minute! We haven't prayed with them!"

And the four of us immediately formed a circle. Standing in our small entryway, beside our washer and dryer, our friends prayed.

They entered into his presence with ease.

They spoke of his blessings.

They worshipped him.

They adored him.

And as we stood and soaked in our friend's conversation with the Lord, I heard two people pray who had never given up on their son and never walked away from their Father.

Certainly doubt entered when a son who was an answer to their prayers became a son who was the source of unfathomable grief.

Jesus himself, while hanging on the cross, cried out: "My God, my God, why have you forsaken me?"[152]

Our human friends probably had a similar moment in private, but they never waivered in public. Their faith isn't based on their feelings. Their faith is based on their knowledge of Him. They have modeled for me a faith that doesn't stop. A faith that compels them to *keep serving publicly* no matter what is happening privately.

They have demonstrated a relentless faith to countless people that makes my faith pale in comparison.

They " . . . sing of the steadfast love of the Lord, forever; with my mouth I will make known your faithfulness to all generations."[153]

---

[152] Mark 15:34c (ESV)

[153] Psalm 89:1 (ESV)

As I ponder their faithfulness, it urges me to grow mine. Oh, that I would someday have faith like my long-time friends: a faith that doesn't look down at my circumstances during the hard journey, but keeps my eyes up on Jesus *despite* the exhausting journey.

Second, I remember God's promises.

Years ago, I was reading this verse and it became an anchor for me as we found ourselves in this season of life without one of our kids: " . . . I will contend with those who contend with you, and your children I will save."[154] There is a promise that God will save my children!

Scholars write that this verse is implicitly tied to Hosea 3:1-3, when Hosea goes and finds his wife to show his love to her again, despite a separation he did not want and her sin. For the record, I have no doubt my husband and I have sinned in this situation with our Wanderer. Just as Gomer is not blameless in creating the void between herself and her husband, my husband and I are not blameless in creating a void between our son and us. We have tried to tell this son that we love him, but it doesn't seem to be received well. At the very least, he doesn't hear it in his heart.

This verse also promises to "contend with those who contend with me." Dear Lord, when it's my kids who have contended with me—and you are contending with them—please be gentle!

Have you ever pulled your child off the roof of your house? Have you ever stopped a child from jumping

---

[154] Isaiah 49:25b (NIV)

onto a glass table? Have you ever stopped a child from turning on a gas stove?

Yeah . . . we have, too.

We've stopped all these activities in our house because we didn't want our kids injured or, worse, killed. We had more knowledge than our kids. We knew being on the roof of our house wasn't a safe place for a five-year-old. The chances of falling and being killed or suffering serious injury were too great.

How many prayers and requests have we made to our Lord where he just shakes his head and says: not going to happen. In his Word, it's phrased: "You do not know what you are asking."

I believe our Father is denying our requests because he has the entire picture. He knows what will happen if we get what we ask for. Just like the toddlers who don't understand the dangers of the moment, who want to experience things that are ultimately harmful, we adults have limited knowledge of outcomes in life. We must trust God knows what he's doing.

At the right time, God will make it happen.

#SomeMiraclesNeedAMom | #AuthorSMcKeown

Another promise I stand on in this matter is, " . . . At the right time, I'll make it happen."[155] I don't get to decide *when* a miracle will happen. God does. I ultimately have no control over that process.

I can ask.

I can believe.

I can trust.

I can beg and plead.

But God is God.

He's the one who knows far better than I what should be happening in what time frame in this vast world.

Third, allow others to comfort you.

Sharing a walk with a wanderer with family and friends is a shaky tightrope. Some ask. Some don't. Who wants to keep hearing about unfathomable grief? There is an underlying pain that is hard to discuss. But one couple we have known for decades understands too well. They are experiencing it, too.

One day I received a package in the mail from this friend, totally unexpected. It was a necklace with a hand-written card. She wrote, in part: "I know it has been a struggle for you to believe there will be a change in (your son's) heart, and I have that same struggle regarding (our son). I want this necklace to be an encouragement to you as you *Imagine More* for (your son's) life and your relationship with him."

The necklace was on a long silver chain with the words *Imagine More.*

---

[155] Isaiah 60:22 *The Message*, NavPress, 2018 (MSG).

People that understand your circumstances are a gift! This gift meant so much to me because she *got it*. She understood what my husband and I were going through.

To put it simple: when you're not getting your miracle, keep praying. Keep hoping. Keep believing.

In our Leader's neighborhood, there is a tree that blooms later in the spring than all other trees. This particular tree stands out—alone—beautifully blossoming after all others have turned to green leaves.

Perhaps our Wanderer is a late bloomer, much like that tree? Maybe he'll realize—as most kids do eventually—that mom and dad are okay after all?

We can hope.

Last fall, my family was sitting around playing a game in our living room. The premise of the game was to guess which kid had which characteristics as children. For example: which kid was the most daring? Which kid liked to sleep the most? Our Princess was getting a few of the answers wrong. When I told her the correct answers, that it was the Wanderer with the characteristic in question, she said something that made my heart ache: "I don't know (that brother)!" I hadn't even thought about it. He moved out of our house to go to college when she was only four years old. He had been home one summer and visited rarely until the visits stopped completely. Of course she doesn't know this brother! But I hadn't realized it until she voiced it.

244

What else haven't we realized?

On a final note, in the scheme of things, does it really matter if we see our son and his family on Earth again? It. Does. Not. Where we really want to see them is in heaven. We don't bargain with our God, i.e., "If we can't see them here on Earth, at least let us see them in heaven." But we pray for the Lord to remind our son of the faith he had as a child and for a desire to return to that faith, if indeed he is away from it.

I would die for *any* of my kids. Jesus taught me how: "For here is the way God loved the world—he gave his only, unique Son *as a gift*. So now everyone who believes in him will never perish but experience everlasting life." [156]

I now lay down what *I* want, for my son's sake.

I just wish longsuffering didn't take so long to suffer through.

I'm hoping again. It's not easy. There are days my hope wavers a bit. But I'm getting there.

We are taught to take losses with the wins. But this loss has been hard to take.

Throughout this process, my prayers are shifting from selfish prayers, what I want to happen, to eternal prayers. Lord, your will be done on Earth as it is in heaven. We dedicated all of our children to the Lord as infants, now we totally release our Wanderer to him. What will be, will be.

---

[156] 1 John 3:16 (TPT)

Oswald Chambers writes, "Jesus never mentioned unanswered prayer. He had the unlimited certainty of knowing that prayer is always answered . . . Jesus said, ' . . . everyone who asks receives . . .' (Matthew 7:8). Yet we say, 'But . . ., but . . .' God answers prayer in the best way—not just sometimes, but every time.'"[157]

I believe!

His final message to his disciples was to go back to Jerusalem and wait.

While we wait, God works. But, again, waiting can be the hardest thing of all.

Some day, I pray, my husband and I will be able to put behind us the "hope deferred (that) makes the heart sick,"[158] and experience anew ". . . a desire fulfilled (that) is a tree of life."[159]

We will keep praying . . . and believing.

Is your heart sick?

Has hope been deferred too long?

A simple prayer: *Dear Lord, give me strength to continue to hope when reason tells me to give up hoping. In this weak spot, may You be ever strong in me.*

---

[157] Oswald Chambers, *My Utmost for His Highest* (Grand Rapids: Discovery House, 1992), May 26.
[158] Proverbs 13:12a (ESV)
[159] Proverbs 13:12b (ESV)

19

Some Miracles Need a Mom

As you read this final chapter, please keep in mind that the words in this book were written several years after all these things occurred in our family. Similarly, the Gospels were written after Jesus' lifetime. The authors gained tremendous hindsight into what had occurred with that additional time of study, reflection, and understanding. Likewise, I am writing this after my children have all reached adulthood, and the distance of time has given me a better perspective.

Perspectives develop and change over time.

I had no clue what I was doing . . . at first.

I was scared for my kids . . . at first.

I was worried by what the professionals were saying about our kids' many challenges and that their predictions would limit what our kids could accomplish in life . . . at first.

And then I turned to Jesus.

Would our Determined be institutionalized if Jesus didn't teach me how this son learned?

Would Justice be attending the "school of hard knocks" if we hadn't prayed, asking for the Lord to soften his anger?

Would our Princess be married, if I had stayed silent, to a man who refused to be a provider?

Would we ever dare hope to see our Wanderer again?

Would our Leader be the excellent negotiator he is in the business world if he hadn't lived in a household that needed a mediator on a daily basis in our private world?

Would my husband and I still be together if we didn't have a great Arbitrator in the midst of our marriage?

I believe the Lord changed my kids' world as I delved deeper into his.

The Lord changes our kids' world as we delve deeper into his.

#SomeMiraclesNeedAMom | #AuthorSMcKeown

When family life feels so overwhelming and you can't imagine better days, but better days finally arrive, it's a miracle.

The Lord's purposes for our children prevailed.

And as parents, my husband and I grew stronger in the process. We learned to trust in Jesus. We were repeatedly reminded that he has the power to act *however* he deems best.

In her book *Awaken*, Priscilla Shirer writes:

> So today, if your current circumstances are not what you ever imagined they'd be—if your dreams have been dashed and your expectations unmet—if you've been taken captive by life, as if kidnapped into an unfamiliar reality that you'd rather escape—and if you can't understand why anything like this should be happening to you—remember, God has a sovereign plan, and you are a part of it.[160]

You are part of God's sovereign plan for your family!

What our family has been through was not for nothing. God had a plan; this I truly believe. And God used my role as mother in my children's lives to facilitate multiple miracles.

God uses people for many miracles. "Here are some of the parts God has appointed for the church: first

---

[160] Priscilla Shirer, *Awaken* (Nashville: B&H Publishing, 2017).

are apostles, second are prophets, third are teachers, then ***those who do miracles* ...**"[161]

Maybe all moms *do* work miracles.

I know jar fillers do.

I believe God used me as a jar filler for my kids. I did nothing of my own accord.

I did what the Lord told me to do.

He showed me how my kids learned best.

He showed me how to persevere when I wasn't sure of outcomes.

He showed me "what would Jesus do" when I was unsure what to do.

He revealed his Word to me so I could find guidance, concepts, and learn to trust him.

I prayed. He imparted wisdom that I listened to. Then I obeyed.

We don't know exactly when the miracle took place at Cana. Was it as the servants poured the water into the ceremonial vessels? Was it as the master of the banquet brought the cup to his lips? Or was it somewhere in between?

We don't know the exact time.

Neither do my husband and I know the exact time when the miracles took place with our kids.

It all happened somewhere along the journey.

The destination at the end of the journey—the ultimate goal—for our family was that each child would become a functioning member of society. But

---

[161] 1 Corinthians 12:28 New Living Translation (NLT)

that was only part of it. Another dream was that they would function in society—in life—with a *spouse*.

The wedding in Cana was a family celebration. Weddings in modern times are also family celebrations, but maybe they're a bit sweeter when you've been told it's unlikely the event will ever be held for some members of your family.

I remember the day our Determined was first diagnosed with autism. As I was crying in the car, many fears were flashing through my mind. One was that he would never marry. When a wedding day *did* happen for him, the miracle that God worked for this son was never more pronounced for me.

At weddings, strong emotions flow like wine. The parents of the bride or groom reflect on all of the moments that occurred to get the family to this event. From weeks of potty training to countless moments of life training throughout the years, the images fly through our minds as we watch the beaming bride walk down the aisle. That moment is the culmination of the excitement of the day! It's what the bride has dreamed about—and the parents.

God orchestrated numerous miracles for weddings to occur for four of our children (so far)! As a mom, each wedding day felt like the culmination of my sons' individual journeys in many ways.

Our boys each found wives that support them in their chosen careers, agree with them on family goals, and walk with them in Christ.

We believe someday our daughter will also find someone who will support her and tell her, "Everything will be okay." Just like her daddy does for me.

And our boys will be dressed in their best, and our daughter and her intended will be dressed in their best. And their best wedding attire will look good on our kids.

They may not look like much of a miracle from the outside.

But they are.

And miracles look good on our kids!

All of our children face a life in this world that includes problems. And there are always more problems to come. I never expected a perfect existence for my kids here on earth. What I did expect—and fight for—was a level playing field for them so they could participate fully in life.

Amos Yong, in *Zacchaeus: Short and Un-seen,* writes:

> Normate assumptions would have expected Jesus to heal the sick, impaired, and disabled. Jesus does no such thing in this case, although he definitively acknowledges the presence of full health in the sense of salvation for Zacchaeus. On the other hand, the prejudices of the people are confronted, and Jesus' acceptance of Zacchaeus just as he is undermines their expectations that those who are impaired and disabled need to be "fixed" or cured in order to participate fully in the renewal and restoration of Israel.[162]

---

[162] Amos Yong, *Zacchaeus: Short and Un-seen,* Baylor.edu, p. 15-16.

Fixed—as in erasing the problem—or functioning, as in helping in furthering a purpose? I never prayed that my children would be fixed, in essence, healed (perhaps my faith wasn't strong enough), but that they would be functioning in society. I believe wholeheartedly, without reservation, that my many prayers were miraculously answered.

"Be strong and let your heart take courage, all you who wait for the Lord."[163] reveals hope is confidence about what will happen coupled with ignorance about its timing. We don't know how things will turn out in the end. Only God knows for sure. But we can be confident that it will be okay however it turns out.

The Conductor was right!

On the end table beside my comfy chair in my living room is my Bible, along with a variety of books to help me become a better mother and human being. Alternating devotionals get moved there from my numerous piles and bookshelves throughout the house in seasons. I have so much to learn. One of my favorite devotionals is *My Utmost For His Highest* by Oswald Chambers. His entry for April 14 reads, in part:

> . . . the joy of the Lord is your strength (Nehemiah 8:10). Where do the saints get their joy? If we did not know some Christians well, we might think from just observing them that they have no burdens at all to bear. But we must lift the veil from our eyes. The

---

[163] Psalm 31:24 (ESV)

fact that the peace, light, and joy of God is in them is proof that a burden is there as well. The burden that God places on us squeezes the grapes in our lives and produces the wine, but most of us see only the wine and not the burden. No power on earth or in hell can conquer the Spirit of God living within the human spirit; it creates an inner invincibility. If your life is producing a whine, instead of the wine of miracles, then ruthlessly kick it out. It is definitely a crime for a Christian to be weak in God's strength.[164]

One of the miracles in this process is that it changes not only our kids, but us, as well. We transform from mere moms to jar fillers. We are wiser, richer in life experiences, perhaps steadier in the problems that come next, because there are always more problems to come.

But we've hopefully learned the process that squeezes good wine from us, rather than a whine.

Nothing motivates a mom like an arrow of low expectations shot across her baby's stroller. I got passionate about the one who is so passionate about you and me that he died so we could live. Going to the feet of my Lord, standing and fighting for multiple miracles on behalf of my children changed my passion for him. I got serious about pursuing him—not just to obtain a miracle—but also to

---

[164] Oswald Chambers, *My Utmost For His Highest* (Grand Rapids: Discovery House Publishers, 1992, Updated Version), April 14.

maintain a relationship that went far beyond Sunday mornings. I got serious about making more room for my Lord and making it less about myself. In a world of perpetual selfishness, perhaps that's the biggest miracle of them all.

I have described for you, briefly within this book, the moments and miracles in which God was at work within our family. It is impossible for me to describe to you all the miracles that will take place beyond our four walls. They are the unseen miracles. The seen miracles, those now out in the world I call my children, are only seen when you know their beginning struggles.

Our oldest is a talented business consultant, using his natural negotiating skills regularly in the corporate world. But he's also not afraid to use it wherever needed. He and his wife were walking in a large mall in a large city one day and witnessed a commotion. Two men were yelling at each other and were about to come to blows. My son quickly stepped in between, first admonishing both men to calm down; second, he asked what had created the conflict.

The older of the two men shared: "My wife was walking here while I was inside a store, and this guy came along and ran her over while on his skateboard!"

The younger man countered: "I warned her! I yelled for her to move several times!"

The older man said, "She's deaf! She didn't hear you!"

My Leader. Standing in the gap for the silently disabled, yet again.

The Leader's wife comforted the man's injured wife and my son stayed in between the two men until security arrived.

Of course, we know little about our Wanderer at this writing. We believe he is still with the military, traveling the world—perhaps what God had intended all along. Last we heard, he works with satellites, using his strong computer abilities.

At this writing, our Justice is starting his own non-profit, seeking to teach a group he has a special compassion for about the saving grace of Jesus Christ. He is using his own funds from his day job as a salesman to enlighten those in the dark.

Our Determined one graduated from college with a music performance degree—playing that saxophone he'd picked up in sixth grade. But, as a married man, he carried on the fifth-generation tradition of our family to become a railroader.

When Determined was still a preschooler, I feared he would never do so many of the things his siblings did, including walk through our front door and announce, "I'm home!" After he and his wife were married, they moved into our basement while in transition, waiting to take possession of their new home. Not long after, the Conductor's train was traveling one direction on a set of tracks; my son's train was traveling on the adjacent track, heading the opposite direction. The Conductor reports his hand-held radio squawked to life as our son's train passed, and he heard our Determined's voice call out over the radio, "See you at home, Dad." To a world that didn't know the struggles of life this child had in the beginning, this interaction would mean very little. But now that you know how experts predicted his life would be, does it change what you see?

God answered my prayers for our Princess, too. She is a voracious reader. After graduating with an English degree, she landed a job at a publishing house. She gets to read all day long.

But, as previously mentioned, we were privileged to pray with each of them as children, introducing them to the Son of Man, the Savior. The One who began to reveal himself at that little wedding in Cana. The One, we, in turn, as parents, were honored to introduce our children to.

The four we are in relationship with each attend church regularly, continuing to pursue a Lord that never changes in this ever-changing world.

Our miracles have grown and spread—literally across the country. My kids' lives are touching others, and those lives will touch others. And the miracles will keep going, compounding the miracles that happened in our little brick house on Mulberry Street.

Fear is the number one thing that you must fight as you pursue a miracle. Don't allow it! Don't miss out!

I sing of the Lord's many answered prayers! "Glory to God in the highest, and on earth peace among those with whom he is pleased!"[165]

---

[165] Luke 2:14 (ESV)

A Blessing

"God is our refuge and strength, a very present help in trouble. Therefore we will not fear though the earth gives way, though the mountains be moved into the heart of the sea, though its waters roar and foam, though the mountains tremble at its swelling."[166]

Though everything around us seems to be crumbling into despair—God is our refuge and strength. We only are truly in deep trouble when we *forget* that he's there.

Remember God!

Remember that you are the best person to pursue a miracle for your family!

And remember . . . some miracles need a mom.

---

[166] Psalm 46:1-3 (ESV)

Epilogue

In the last chapter, I wrote: "There are always more troubles to come."

I just didn't expect them to come so soon.

Four days after finishing the last draft of this book, my husband passed away very unexpectedly from an undiagnosed brain aneurysm at the age of sixty-four. Forty-one years of married life was suddenly over.

I was numb, in shock, but what my husband and I had practiced for years, doing life with others, became a lifeline.

Several friends I mentioned in earlier chapters were gathered for a weekend at a lake several hours away when they received the news of the Conductor's passing. We were talking on the phone later, through the speaker, when I heard one of the gals whisper in the background: *Should we tell her?*

Tell me what? I demanded.

Oh, you heard that? Someone responded: *We're all packed. We're driving up to come to you. We'll be there tonight.*

My friends, people the Conductor and I had done life with for several years, were coming in the midst of one of my greatest times of need. Our friends—with whom we had dined, laughed, raised rascals, worked side-by-side in the community and in the church—they were dropping everything to come and steady my world that had just been rocked.

And they cried with me.

Later, when the pastor we served under the longest came with his wife to the house, and he leaned in to give an appropriate hug, he asked, "How are you doing?" And I responded, "Hyperventilating." As he finished leaning in, his words were a whisper, and I heard, "We've got 'ya."

We've got 'ya.

Those words were a balm to a shocked soul.

My local kids all came. We cried together and then they rolled up their sleeves and started working. I wrote the program and the obituary for my husband's memorial and I chose the music to be played, but my kids (including very talented daughters-in-law!) did everything else. It was such a proud mom moment to watch my kids band together and "get 'er done."

I was numb those first couple of weeks. And then everyone went home. And the numbness wore off.

And the deep, chest-pounding pain of loss became achingly apparent.

But I was not alone.

I picked up my favorite devotional, read my bible, and turned on Pandora. And steeped myself in the presence of my Lord.

As I clung to Him, He reminded me of a particular passage in His Word: When I was in distress, I sought the Lord; at night I stretched out untiring hands and my soul refused to be comforted. I remembered you, O God, and I groaned; I mused, and my spirit grew faint. You kept my eyes from closing; I was too troubled to speak. I thought about the former days, the years of long ago; I remembered my songs in the night. My heart mused and my spirit inquired: "Will the Lord reject us forever? Will he never show his favor again? Has his unfailing love vanished forever? Has his promise failed for all time? Has God forgotten to be merciful? Has he in anger withheld his compassion?" Then I thought, "To this I will appeal: the years of the right hand of the Most High." **I will remember the deeds of the Lord; yes, I will remember your miracles of long ago. I will meditate on all your works, and consider all your mighty deeds.**[167]

Yes, I will remember what the Lord has done. He was there for our family when each of the three children was diagnosed with less-than-stellar outcomes. He was there for us when sleepless nights and drawn-out days were seemingly and endlessly back-to-back. He was there for us when we turned to Him because we didn't know what else to do.

My story has changed. My God has not.

---

[167] Psalm 77:2-12 (NIV)

My story has changed. My God has not.

#SomeMiraclesNeedAMom | #AuthorSMcKeown

And . . . "I remain confident of this: I will see the goodness of the Lord in the land of the living. Wait for the Lord; be strong and take heart and wait for the Lord."[168]

Is it a coincidence that one of the few characteristics of Mary's I didn't focus on in the previous chapters was this: Mary. Was. A. Widow. She wasn't walking through life with a spouse who balanced her, who cherished her, who took care of all the household things that weren't in her skill set. She didn't have a guy that checked on her when she was sick, who protected her, who cherished her. But what she did have was a relationship with the Son of Man. She relied on the wisdom she had learned from Him. This I believe.

And as Mary mourned Joseph, was she possibly remembering his strong hands that caught her Baby as she delivered in less than ideal circumstance?

Was she remembering how his skilled hands made beautiful things out of wood?

---

[168] Psalm 27:13-14 (ESV)

Was she remembering how patient and loving her husband had been?

I think she was. I think she was pondering, once again; this time, on what a wonderful husband God had given her.

As He gave me, as well.

My Conductor did countless things for me. My friends and family agree: the Conductor spoiled me!

Do you mean every wife's gas tank doesn't magically get filled on its own?

Do you mean every wife's husband doesn't cook wonderful meals, often?

Do you mean every wife's husband doesn't do the things the wife dislikes doing, just because he naturally likes to help?

He was so good at caring for others. In fact, he was gifted at it. As I wrote in chapter 16, " . . . of the Conductor stating his children were his hobby. That's how he lived . . . He put down his golf clubs and played with his kids. His involvement with our kids will affect our family for generations to come. Of that, I have no doubt."

He cared for family, friends, and even the passengers on his train and co-workers. He showed all of us who knew him how to care for the people around us.

All those things that he did for me, I now struggle to learn to do for myself. It's time to put on my big girl pants, don the moniker of Steel Magnolia, and lean on my Lord like never before. In chapter 17, I wrote: "Her (Mary's) role as the mother of Jesus was not easy, but she grew in her faith through the difficulties she endured." Dear Lord, through this newest season, may my faith grow as well.

My Lord has been teaching me to get comfortable in the alone time with just Him and me. To not need the constant cacophony of kids, grandkids, and busy activity to numb my feelings, but to rely on my Lord's presence to strengthen me to grow past the many tumultuous emotions, to learn to be content in the "be still."

As I grow through this mourning period, I am reminded of my sister-in-law's demand as she was wheeled into surgery: "This better not take long, I have feet to wash!"

I am at the point in my grief, "Lord, this better not take long! I have people to help!"

My four-year-old granddaughter asked her mom, after a book was read to her about heaven, "Mommy, can I go to heaven and visit Papa and come back?" And when that was gently denied her, "When I die, I'm gonna see Papa!"

Are *you* looking forward to heaven?

There are so many things I learned through the many years raising my children. One thing that I haven't always been good at was to tell my kids what the Lord has done. After the Israelites crossed the Jordan, they were instructed to place rocks at the river's edge to remind the generations of the things God had done.

I have many rocks to place.

I remember the peace I felt after the Conductor's last bicycle accident, and that as I had learned to achieve peace, I needed to praise God. Jeff Deyo, a contemporary Christian music artist and worship leader, preaches: "Praising God doesn't change God, it changes us."

I remember that two are better than one, and that the gift of our friends so many years ago is definitely a gift that keeps on giving.

I remember Priscilla Shirer's quote in chapter 19: "God has a sovereign plan, and you are a part of it." I don't know what God's plan is, but I believe I'm part of what He's doing in my little part of the world. He is God and I trust Him.

Three weeks after the Conductor died, I read the entry for that morning in *My Utmost for His Highest*. " ... Elijah went up by a whirlwind into heaven. And Elisha ... saw him no more."

I ran for my highlighter and noted these lines in this entry:

It is not wrong for you to depend on your "Elijah" for as long as God gives him to you.

You now have to put to the test what you learned when you were with your "Elijah."

If you remain true to what you learned while with your "Elijah," you will receive a sign, as Elisha did, that God is with you.

Make a determination to trust in God, and do not even look for Elijah anymore.[169]

---

[169] Oswald Chambers, *My Utmost For His Highest* (Grand Rapids: Discovery House Publishers, 1992, Updated Version),

My Conductor had taught me so much.

As I followed the advice learned, determined to trust in God, I continued to read my favorite devotional. Eight months later, I came across this: "Living a life of faith means never knowing where you are being led." Further down, on the same day: "A life of faith is not a life of one glorious mountaintop experience after another, like soaring on eagles wings, but is a life of day-in and day-out consistency; a life of walking without fainting."[170]

". . . To whom much was given, of him much will be required . . ."[171] I feel the "much" especially now as I parent alone. I have been given much, but there is much required. The Conductor, as previously mentioned, was the favorite parent—and rightfully so. I kept the kids alive with the mundane everyday tasks while he was out of town working. He came home and, after getting some sleep, was ready to play.

I miss his guidance: his hand silently reaching under a table and resting on my leg, the message loud and clear: "Cool it, leave that subject alone."

Now, to curb my desire to be right and point out truths, I need to listen to the Holy Spirit telling me, "Leave that subject alone."

Problems really *are* opportunities for growth!

A Universal Pictures film titled *An American Tail* was released in 1986. When it became available for

August 11.

[170] Oswald Chambers, *My Utmost For His Highest* (Grand Rapids: Discovery House Publishers, 1992, Updated Version), March 19.

[171] Luke 12:48 (ESV)

home viewing, we purchased it for our kids. There is a scene in the movie when the main character (Fievel, a mouse) is lost. He sings a mournful song as he thinks of his papa. At the same time, his papa thinks of him—and they both look at the full moon as they think of each other, unable to communicate; yet, longing for each other.

Our kids had been watching this newly purchased motion picture as the Conductor was getting ready, once again, to leave for work. Just before heading out the door, this time on New Year's Eve morning, he said, "Exactly at midnight, look out the window at the moon. I promise, wherever I'm at on the train, I will look at the moon, too. We can't talk to each other, but we'll be thinking of each other. Love you!"

I remembered this instance just a few weeks ago, and then the Lord prompted me, "You still have the same focus."

Of course! The focus has changed, but we are still focusing on the same thing!

I am maintaining my focus, my concentration, on my Lord. And I believe my Conductor is, too. He's just got a better vantage point from where he's at.

This was a great comfort to me!

The Conductor is looking at Jesus from his new home in heaven; I am staying focused on Jesus from Earth. And we are still thinking of each other.

A few years before the Conductor died, as we were riding in the car in silence, he blurted out: "I don't believe I'm going to see (our Wanderer) on this earth again."

My response to his statement was akin to "oh, ye, of little faith." But, again, the Conductor was right. He didn't see this son the last eight years of his life. We can't regain those years here on Earth, but I still have hope that we will all be together again. Someday.

The Conductor's mother used to say, as she'd shake her head, commenting about the Conductor: "I don't know how that boy is still alive." At one point, he'd even come home and announced *once again*: "I was almost killed at work today." And I reacted, "My heart can't take these announcements! Please, I promise to pray for you, but I just can't hear about your close calls any longer." Looking back, my husband's guardian angels had been working overtime for years. May they finally get some much-needed rest.

Many years ago, a man at our church approached me after we had worked together on a team. He was originally from Africa, and had some African wisdom for me. In his pronounced French accent, he proclaimed: "Sandy, *you* are an African woman. You are a big woman with a big personality and a big laugh. If you ever get to Africa, Sandy, they're going to love you."

I told him not to hold his breath, it would probably never happen.

Yet, over a decade later, I found myself being invited to travel to Africa with a team of women to help put on a leadership conference for women. However, I got sick at the last moment and wasn't able to go. The Conductor, as usual, had written me a card with plans to secretly insert it into my luggage before I left for the airport so I would find it when I got to my hotel room. Since I was no longer able to go on the trip, he presented it to me at home. After his death just five months later, I came across the card again and was astonished by the words he'd written and their seemingly new meaning:

Every day I will pray for you and your team. I will miss you but know you are serving as <u>He</u> needs. You have fun and be sure to laugh like an African Woman. I love you~

There was no way he knew he was leaving this earth so soon, but somehow a hand-written note that hinted at an eternal mindset and these coming years of a forced, yet temporary, separation were comforting.

It was his last "love note" to me, but it is also like an encouragement for the days ahead: *You have fun and be sure to laugh.*

I'll miss you, my Conductor, but it's not *goodbye*. It's only *see you later*.

This, I believe.

The pastor that drove ten hours to come and do the memorial service for us knew the Conductor and our immediate family well. While doing prep work for the service, he asked me what some of the Conductor's favorite Bible verses were. I told him I didn't know because my husband had switched over years before to using a free Bible app on his phone. I couldn't go to a physical Bible and see what was highlighted. So, we were "pinch hitting" in this regard. However, the pastor had invited our kids to share in writing, and the Leader shared a verse that I found a couple weeks *after* the service highlighted in a note on the Conductor's phone. Coincidence? I don't think so. The Conductor had made the notation for that same verse *two weeks* before he died:

> For this reason I kneel before the Father, from whom his whole family in heaven and on earth derives its name. I pray that out of his glorious riches he may strengthen you with power through his Spirit in your inner being, so that Christ may dwell in your hearts through faith. And I pray that you, being rooted and established in love, may have power, together with all the saints, to grasp how wide and long and high and deep is the love of Christ, and to know this love that surpasses knowledge—that you may be filled to the measure of all the fullness of God. Now to him who is able to do immeasurably more than all we ask or imagine, according to his power that is at work within us, to him be glory in the church and in Christ Jesus throughout all generations, for ever and ever. Amen.[172]

To Him be the glory.

We have a pond in back of our house. The Conductor, and any family members that were around, would

---

[172] Ephesians 3:14-20 (NIV)

shovel off the snow and use it as an ice skating rink. It had become a tradition for our Christmases back in Minnesota. Of course, growing up in Minnesota, the Conductor was a good ice skater! In his younger days, he had battled on the ice hockey rink for hours with his cousins.

But in this season of life, it was a little gentler. When our oldest granddaughter was just learning to skate, her papa took her hands and skated with her. He gently twirled her on the ice, and guided her over the bumps of the ice, expertly guiding her to skate backwards, then gave her a gentle push toward her mom, watching from the sideline. As she safely got to her mother's arms, she excitedly exclaimed: "Mom, did you see! I didn't know I could skate so good!"

It's such an example of the Conductor: strength, gentleness, and endurance. He liked to be in the background. And he made the rest of us look *and feel* like we could do more than we thought we could.

Last Christmas everyone stood on the ice for a picture. The sound of the picture being taken was followed *immediately* by the sound of the ice cracking beneath our feet. Everyone scattered in different directions, screaming and laughing, running to solid ground. It was instinctive. We all knew we needed to get to solid ground without even thinking about it.

We're standing on solid ground today, with our Savior, because the Conductor expertly, but gently, and with endurance, guided this family to Him.

Acknowledgements

This is not a project that was accomplished alone. Thank you to my beta readers:

Rev. Dr. Lon Kvanli and the Rev. Dr. Heidi Kvanli, my brother and sister-in-law. Their thoroughness, patience, and wisdom were invaluable to me.

Dr. Raul Sanchez and his wife, Stacy, who were not only beta readers, but walked some of the darkest days with our family as we lived this story.

And, Pastor Tom Jacobs, who has always used his God-given gift of encouragement, to coach us through the multiple years of hard parenting and remind us the answer to our problems was always to move closer to Jesus.

Thank you to my two wise and ever-patient editors/writing coaches, as well: Angie Peters and Anna Henke. You are both 'A-one' in my book!

A big thank you to my five kids, who gave me great material for this book but also gave me many opportunities to grow with the challenges presented.

And, finally, to my husband. He lived this story but never read the last half before passing away suddenly. He wanted the names changed throughout this book, in part, "to protect the not-so-innocent" of this story. But he also never wanted the limelight. As he stands in the light of the Lord, I have no doubt he's hearing, "Well done," from his Lord.

Thanks, Conductor, for being so extremely patient with me, for loving me even when you knew me really, really well, and for being my rock in this chaotic world. See you someday soon.

About the Author

In fifth grade, Sandy's teacher gave the class a writing assignment that changed the trajectory of her life. After turning hers in, Sandy's teacher requested to speak with her privately, asking from where she had copied the story. Sandy said she had not copied it, and, in fact, shared how she got the idea for the story. The teacher's face lit up and responded, "Sandy, you're a writer!"

The seed of a dream was planted that day, but Sandy doubted her dreams of writing while she and her husband raised five children, three with extra challenges. But those forty years of having kids under their roof was a treasure trove of many heart-touching and often humorous stories. She's shared a few of those stories in the multiple anthologies she's contributed to over the years.

Sandy also uses her storytelling skills as a public speaker and continues to pursue her passion for mentoring women, helping others discover that raising children and keeping their marriages strong simultaneously is possible. The story of how Sandy has accomplished much for her family despite her many weaknesses is an extraordinary example for all.

And he said to me, "My grace is sufficient for you,

for my power is made perfect in weakness."

Therefore I will boast all the more gladly about my weaknesses,

so that Christ's power may rest on me."

[2 Corinthians 12:9]